Melodic Forms
The Sculpture of
David Chamberlain

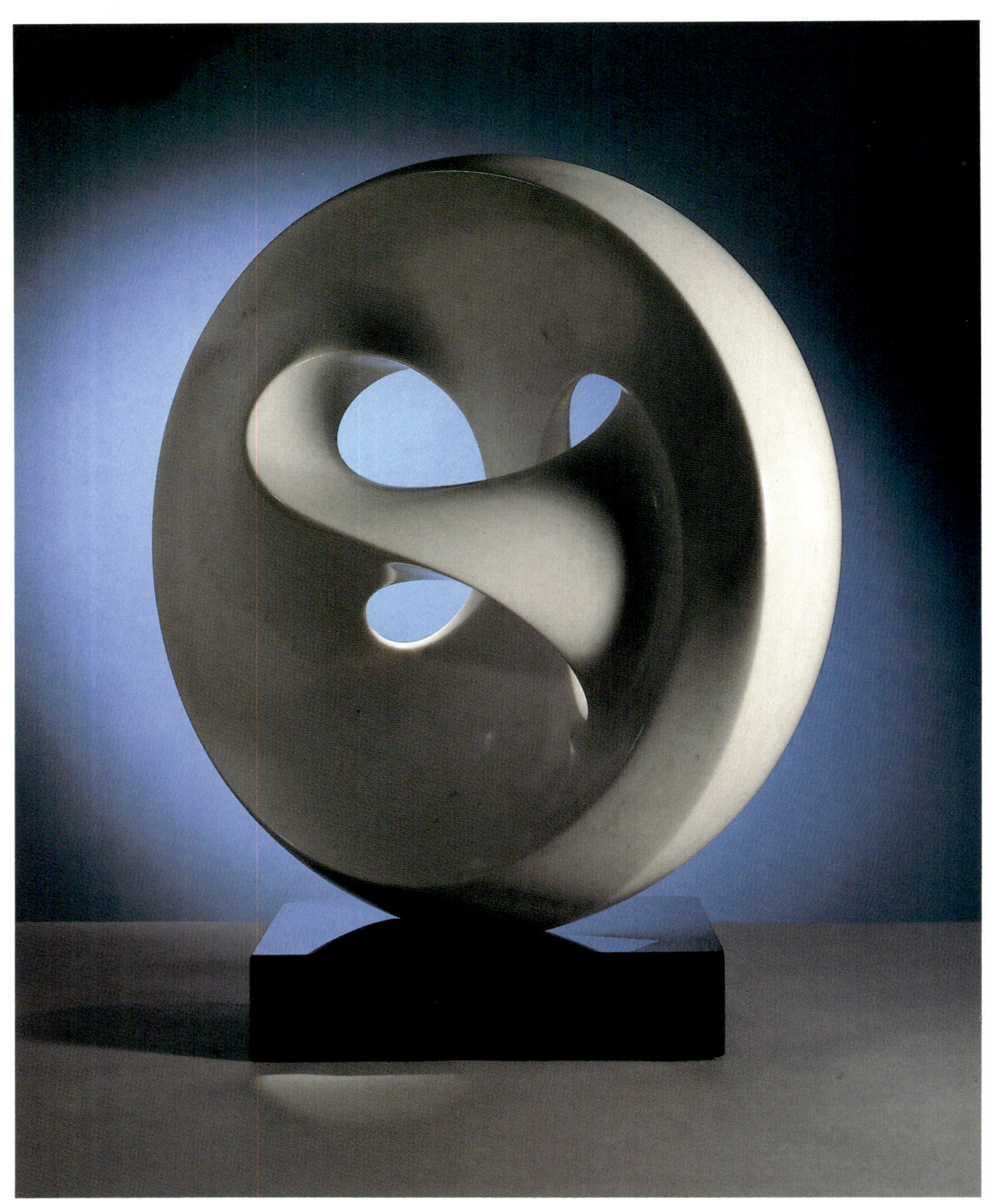

Melodic Forms
The Sculpture of
David Chamberlain

David R. Godine, Publisher
and
Pucker Safrai Gallery
BOSTON

Editor	PAMELA WOLFSON
Designer	DONNA ASPRINIO
Photography	DAVID N. ISRAEL, BOSTON, MASSACHUSETTS

Other Photography   ALPHONSE MICCICHE, SAMUELS STUDIO, MAYNARD, MASSACHUSETTS
RODNEY CHALK, MYSTIC, CONNECTICUT
BETSY CORSIGLIA, MARTHA'S VINEYARD, MASSACHUSETTS
SEAN FARREN, BOSTON, MASSACHUSETTS
DAVID GIBSON, HARTFORD, CONNECTICUT

Studio Assistants   PAUL MILLER
GWEN P. MURPHY
DANIEL FASSETT
JOYCE WATSON
KEVIN AND SCOTT VRABLIK

Artistic/Technical Support
Bronzes   TALLIX ART FOUNDRY, BEACON, NEW YORK
Marbles   GAWET MARBLE COMPANY, RUTLAND, VERMONT
Mahoganies   PALMER AND PARKER HARDWOODS, TEWKSBURY, MASSACHUSETTS
GIBSON, MCILVAIN COMPANY, WHITEMARSH, MARYLAND

First Published in 1990 by
DAVID R. GODINE PUBLISHERS, INC.
Horticultural Hall
300 Massachusetts Avenue
Boston, Massachusetts 02115

PUCKER ART PUBLICATIONS
Pucker Safrai Gallery, Inc.
171 Newbury Street
Boston, Massachusetts 02116

Copyright © 1990 by Pucker Safrai Gallery, Inc.
Sculptures copyright © 1990 by David Chamberlain

LIBRARY OF CONGRESS CATALOGING IN PUBLICATION DATA

Chamberlain, David
Melodic forms : the sculpture of David Chamberlain / edited by
Pamela Wolfson.
p.   cm.
ISBN 0-87923-854-2
1. Chamberlain, David—Themes, motives.   I. Wolfson, Pamela.
II. Pucker-Safrai Gallery.   III. Title.
NB237.C425A4   1990
730'.92—dc20   90-34247
CIP

First edition
Printed in Hong Kong by South China Printing Co. (1988) Ltd.

Foreword

In our century painting has been the art form associated with modernism. More than printmaking, ceramics or sculpture, it is painting that the public most often identifies with the creation of new and uniquely contemporary art. Sculpture is different somehow. After all, sculpture is a difficult medium for museums and galleries to exhibit and even more difficult for curators and critics to interpret. And for the artist, sculpture is complex and arduous to make. It is not surprising, then, that before 1914 there were few pieces of important sculpture being created. Even after that date, much of the sculpture produced was overshadowed by the aesthetics and facility of painting.

One of the most exciting developments during the past 50 years has been the emergence of a strong tradition of modern sculpture. Alexander Calder, Henry Moore and David Smith each developed a personal aesthetic based on the true nature of three-dimensional form. They have been followed by Isamu Noguchi, Anthony Caro and Alexander Lieberman, to list a few. A survey of the work of these and other artists reveals that in many instances it is sculpture that has made one of the greatest contributions to the growing influence of art on our world. In part, this is because it has an undeniable physical immediacy that confronts the viewer. People relate to sculpture as something with a powerful presence of its own. Its materials also call for a high degree of professional competence on the part of the artist. John Russell has called it the "crusading art."

The staff of the McKissick Museum at the University of South Carolina specifically seeks out art forms and artists that convey the excitement and contemporary issues in today's art. David Chamberlain's sculpture is an excellent example of that kind of creativity. A significant part of the current revival of this art form, his work is thoughtfully conceived and masterfully executed. Elegant, compelling, and sensual, it speaks of the grace and beauty of which art and nature are capable.

LYNN ROBERTSON MYERS
Director
McKissick Museum of Art
Columbia, South Carolina

GEORGE D. TERRY
Former Director
McKissick Museum of Art
Columbia, South Carolina

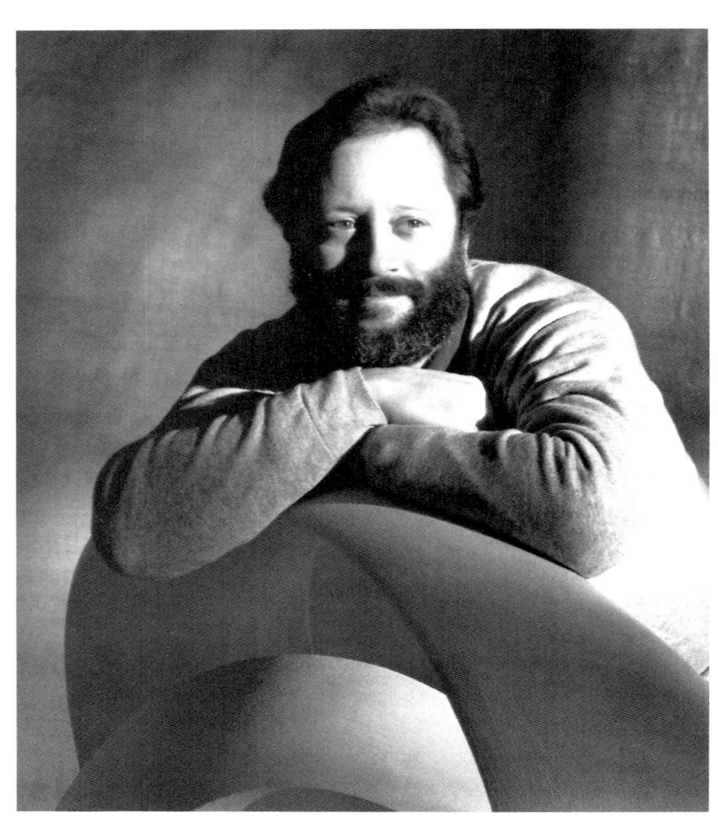

David Chamberlain: Maker of an Elegant Order

Sculpture, like any art, reflects the quality of the artist's mind. In few art forms does this quality stand so naked as in abstract sculpture. We do not see minutiae of life, details of process, or an expression of one philosophic premise. Rather we experience a materialization of the way the artist thinks. The abstract work is a tangible thought, a sensuous revelation, a pattern for the process of both perception and reflection.

As a sculptor, David Chamberlain is attracted to whatever exhibits an elegant simplicity. A line or geometry of elegance can exist in the ideas of physics, in the secreting growth of a seashell, in the tonal progression of a concerto, in the unfolding of a human life. The vitality of his abstract work comes from an expectant perception of the everyday world.

Chamberlain is a man of many enthusiasms. Besides being a sculptor, he is a musician, an architect, and an aspiring pilot. He is comfortable talking about art, computer science, fishing, biology, religion, dance, or business.

It should come as no surprise that Chamberlain is an aviator. He builds and flies the small, ultra-light planes that expose the pilot to the tactile sense of the wind, the pockets of warm and cool air, the eddies and currents of the weather. In such a small craft there is little floorboard beneath one's feet; the only medium between the flyer and the ground is the curling sweep of the wind. And "flyer" is a better word than "pilot" for naming the quality Chamberlain embodies in his work.

A Chamberlain work takes off and flies, swirling into dives and loops. We need only to look carefully at the edge of one of his sculptures. The edge line sails through long wide curves, then dips into a parabolic loop that spins the edge back almost upon itself with centripetal force.

The works give us a genuine feel for movement, a decided aerodynamic force that brings with it a sense of surprise when we go back to the work and realize that what we see is made of rigid material: stone, bronze, wood, gold or ceramic.

Many of Chamberlain's titles come from a love that could be his vocation instead of his avocation. His titles name, in a different lexicon, the same habit of mind: the quick loop or the long wide curve. *Fantasia* and *Rhapsody* suggest free or improvised musical work that runs quickly and lightly. *Nocturne* and *Sarabande* suggest long sustained sweeps. Other names suggest his interest in curling or languorous natural forms: *Eschelle*, *Embryons*, or the poisson series.

Nothing about Chamberlain's art is purely a product of the unconscious mind, though the flow of the lines does sometimes suggest the sinuous languor of reverie or dream. Even the casual viewer is aware of a precision and elegance that is planned and executed with exquisite detail.

Chamberlain reports that he always wanted to be an artist, even as a child. But when he had to make the decision a reality, he looked at science, design, medicine, music, and sculpture. And, of course, he came back to his original choice - because he felt that sculpture would be the most challenging career, that it required of him intellectual as well as physical exertion, that it was sensuous as well as cognitive.

Sculpture is a difficult art. It requires an ability to imagine in three dimensions, even — Chamberlain would say — to imagine in the fourth dimension: time. A sculptor must not only be able to see every angle, he must also be able to see how our eye travels over time. Like the composer of a concerto, the sculptor must provide variety that seems surprising and at the same time inevitable. He must provide strong visual excitement from every possible angle.

For the sculptor, there is no place to hide. The eye of the viewer is relentless. It may begin at almost any place. Though a work has climaxes — places of great exhilaration — it has no beginning, middle, or end. The movement of the eye across time is important, but time is linear only in a limited way. In sculpture there is no backward or forward, and the eye can travel either way along a line that defines an edge. Even the line may turn back upon itself so that the time in the sculpture is self-contained.

Poisson D'Or, Number 15 is a good example of contained movement. The eye can begin anywhere: at the top of the sail-like projection, in the space defined by the ebony paisley, in the curve of the paisley itself, on the red surface below it, in the broad form that defines the larger space, on the outside edges, on the inside edges. But wherever the eye begins, it travels — around curving edges, dipping into the mahogany sheen of the concave planes, latching onto the lines that define the spaces. As long as the eye is willing to play, it is alternately shot out in elation along an elliptical orbit to the edge of the work and brought back into the mounting tension of its center.

We see only one view of *Poisson* in the photograph, but if we imagine the piece 45 degrees to the left, our experience changes. The upper space disappears behind its lip and the involute structure of the ebony paisley becomes clearer as the lower space becomes deeper and more dramatic. The bottom point becomes less pronounced and the top point sharper. Yet we still make the same exciting tour of volumes and surfaces, of planes and spaces, a tour that has duration but is in no way as dictatorial as chronological time.

The title seems to derive less from the shape of the animal it names than from the medium in which the fish swims. The fish experiences its world in swirling currents, in gradual or sudden temperature changes, in the pressure of the water on its body and fins, and the sculptor is giving us, in the shape of wood, the movement of the fish's sensory world.

Chamberlain is also treating us, in this work, to time in another way. Imagine *Poisson* in a light other than the one shown in the photograph, say the light of the pre-sun dawn, when shadows are subtle and edges less pronounced. The poisson swims in a suspended languor as the tension between edges and shadows relaxes.

Though time is linear, the human psyche recognizes in cyclical events a certain time-stamped recurrence that takes on an archetypal resonance. Night has such a resonance. Chamberlain suggests this type of order in *Nocturne*. The Chamberlain gestalt is nothing if not sensuous, and the magic of *Nocturne* is the way it draws us into the recesses of its deep green patina. The surface is as smooth as oil, and the matte, mottled in black, green, and umber, softens the hard bronze surface. The musical compositions called by the same name evoke the thought and feeling of the night, and this piece concentrates on the quiet luxury of the darkness, its warm, dark heft and its deeply recessed orifices, which shelter the body and arouse the libido.

The spaces in this work, swirling in the convolutions of time, have the organic feel of the openings of the aorta or the canal ducts of the inner ear - images appropriate to the ambiance of the night. Yet the openings are purified of what Yeats would call the "blood and mire," placing the reality of the piece in the "artifice of eternity," the kingdom of art that breaks the "bitter furies" of the aggression of time against passion and rest. The "nocturne" of this piece is not one night, but the ever-returning night, its ambiance and sensibility.

Sarabande attacks the nature of time in another way. The lines that spin back upon themselves are missing in this work. Instead the burnished edges almost touch, the way men and women in the separate curving lines of the eighteenth century court dance called the sarabande touched for a moment and then were spun apart in their separate trajectories. The trajectories terminate abruptly within the sculpture, suggesting the music's end.

The interiors of this work are mirror-finished, brilliant like the tone of the clarina, the valveless, soprano trumpet, popular in the era of the sarabande. The polish creates a sumptuous effect contained within the epic stateliness of the hyperbolic curves. No space in this work is completely enclosed, as the spaces are in "Nocturne" or in the poisson pieces. The edges that would form the space are cut sharply at the base or in a flat plane at the top of the work. But the light, reflecting off the courtly mirrored interior, creates its own dark curves which echo the dark granular exterior. In *A Toccata of Galuppi's*, Browning invokes in the concrete setting of the merchant-king carnivals of Venice the same brilliance and gaiety of music and dance, a gaiety existing in time which is always cut short.

Chamberlain's wife, Patrishya, is a ballet dancer, and dance never seems far removed from the play of his work, even when the title given to a piece in no way connotes the movement of bodies. *Embouchure* is one such work. The piece is a matte-finish, cream colored ceramic that spirals in upon itself before it leaps slantwise, creating a bridge to a mass that seems more earthbound. The creamy matte makes the movement — though no less dramatic — more subtle, less splendid than the bold contrasts between the brilliant golden brass and the bark-textured, outer patina of *Sarabande*. Even the broad expanses of this piece seem light, and the edges, while no less delineated, seem less cutting than *Sarabande*'s burnished curves. But the leap and the lightness of touch also evoke the spirit of dance, a dance less formal, more spontaneous than the one in *Sarabande*. The uniformity of the surface finish concentrates the viewer's attention on the effect of light and shadow so that, though subtle, each movement of line and curve is clean and crisp, like the effortless flight of a powerful dancer.

Embouchure also resonates with sensuality, the slantwise leap traveling either outward or inward, depending on the movement of the eye — away from or toward a sheltering concave nest. The leap inward also creates what can perhaps be called an "implied space." The strip or bridge that moves inward curves back upon itself, creating from some viewing angles the appearance of a space, the kind of space the viewer comes to expect in a Chamberlain work. But in this case, the space is the effect created by a three-dimensional Mobius-like strip that rotates 180 degrees as it turns sharply back, veering in the play of dance over itself. At certain angles, the viewer looks into the vortex of a spiral and sees only a hole.

Many of Chamberlain's works, especially those created in 1983, exhibit a fascination with a Mobius-like spiral. The effect, however, is quite different in each, depending not only on the material from which it was composed and its finish, but also on the volume of space its bulk displaces. The range includes works as different as the delicate, mirror bronze *Mazurka* and the sturdy, whirling *Sinfonietta*. The slender flame of *Concerto for Strings* is a lightly coiled spiral, and *Eschelle* a tighter, more elaborately coiled one. Though it shares the apparent simple elegance of all Chamberlain works, *Festivale* is a yet more elaborate play with openings or vortexes than are the spiraling compositions. *Festivale* creates its effects through the rotation of planes around real and implied openings. If you look carefully at the photograph, you will see that the two apparent openings are actually one foreground space that is spliced by a bridge through its center, a bridge that does not connect with the opposite side of the opening. Instead, this bridge also veers to the side, creating the top wing of the sculpture's sail-shaped base. The bridge also creates the top of a lower opening, which can be seen through the foreground aperture.

Festivale is a series of movements within movements, of vistas that surprise and bewitch the eye. And when you turn the work or walk around it, the openings disappear or change position. Light bounces from the edges and concave curves, giving the dark planes shapeliness and energy. The velocity of the return edge at each of the three points suggests the vibrancy of people in celebration.

Fantasia, Cadenza, Rhapsody, and *Entrechat,* also play with a space or spaces that appear, from some angles, to divide into smaller spaces. Are there three apertures in *Entrechat* or one? If we were Lilliputians looking down from just inside the upper aperture, how would we experience the red satin recess in which we stand?

Nocturne is the earliest example of a work with the lipped apertures and sweeping sail-like peaks. Some, such as *Moku No Kaze* and *Lullaby,* when seen straight on into the opening seem focused on absence. Yet always in a Chamberlain work, the opening can also be defined as a "recess," a space that suggests shelter and enclosed safety. Broad is the way and somewhat overpowering the immensity of the scoop-like projection that leads the eye into the calm at the center of *Moku No Kaze.* The center is all the more sheltering for providing a way out that seems impossible when the eye is being herded into the recess.

David Chamberlain's works are tactile poems, existing in dimensions and taking their genesis from the shape within the habit of mind of the sculptor. Only a few are described in this preface. Most are left for us to enter. In the printed format, they require a little more of us, require that we imagine angles and dimensions only hinted at in the single view of a photograph.

But the ordering mind of the sculptor is a broad mind. It has experienced the palpable essence of many realities and, therefore, leaves room for many avenues of entrance. As these pieces enter our consciousness, our experiences of the world at large may begin to take a Chamberlain shape.

In *The Idea of Order at Key West,* Wallace Stevens concerns himself with how the artist — in this case, a woman singing at the edge of the beach — gives a shape to the world:

> It was her voice that made
> The sky acutest at its vanishing.
> She measured to the hour its solitude.
> She was the single artificer of the world
> in which she sang. And when she sang, the sea,
> whatever self it had, became the self
> that was her song, for she was the maker.

The simplicity and elegance of David Chamberlain's sculptures are intoxicating. As a maker of elegant forms, he offers images of truth and beauty in an often rough and complex world.

— JACQUELINE MALONE

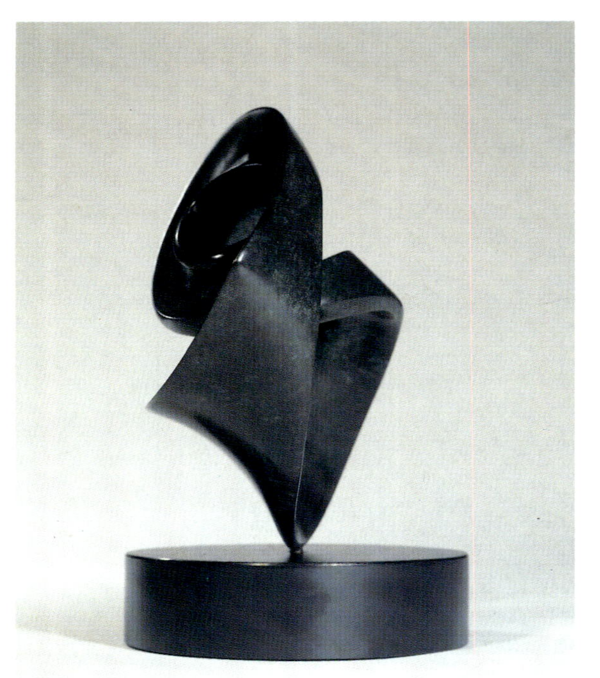

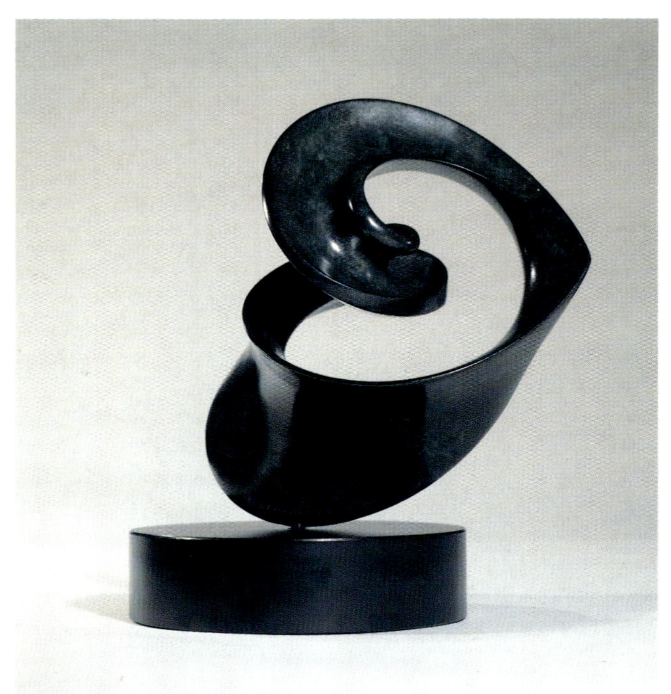

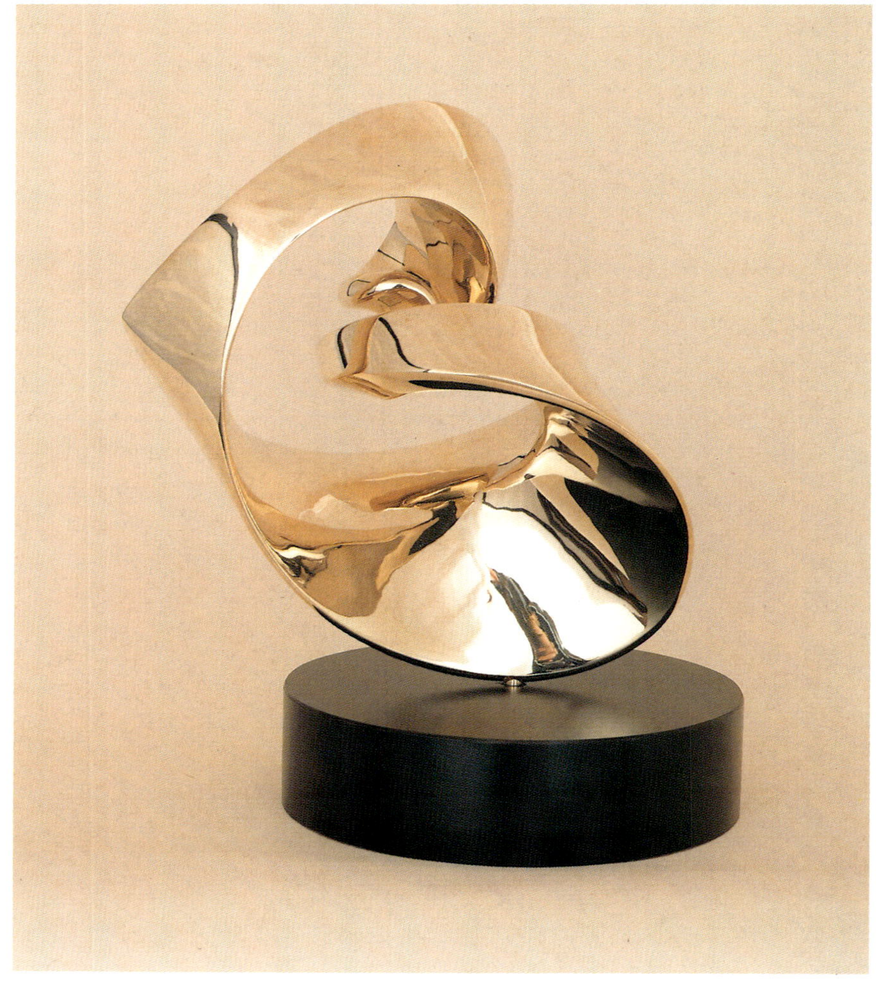

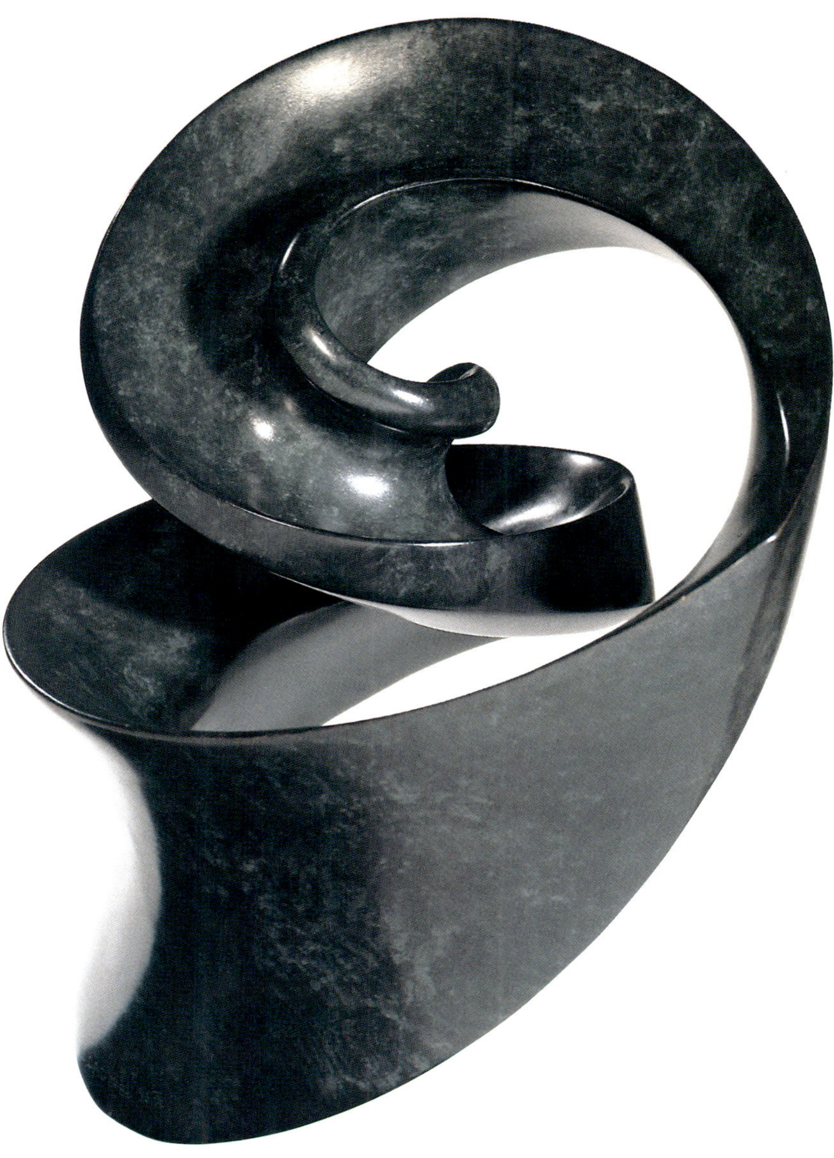

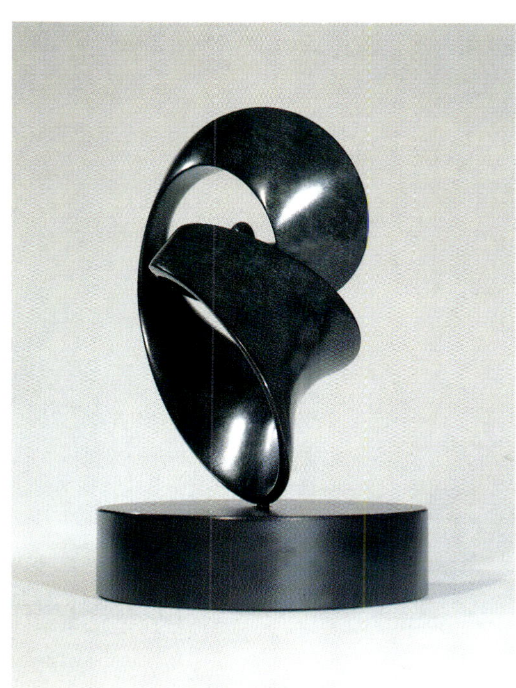

1. BLUMIN'
Patinated bronze

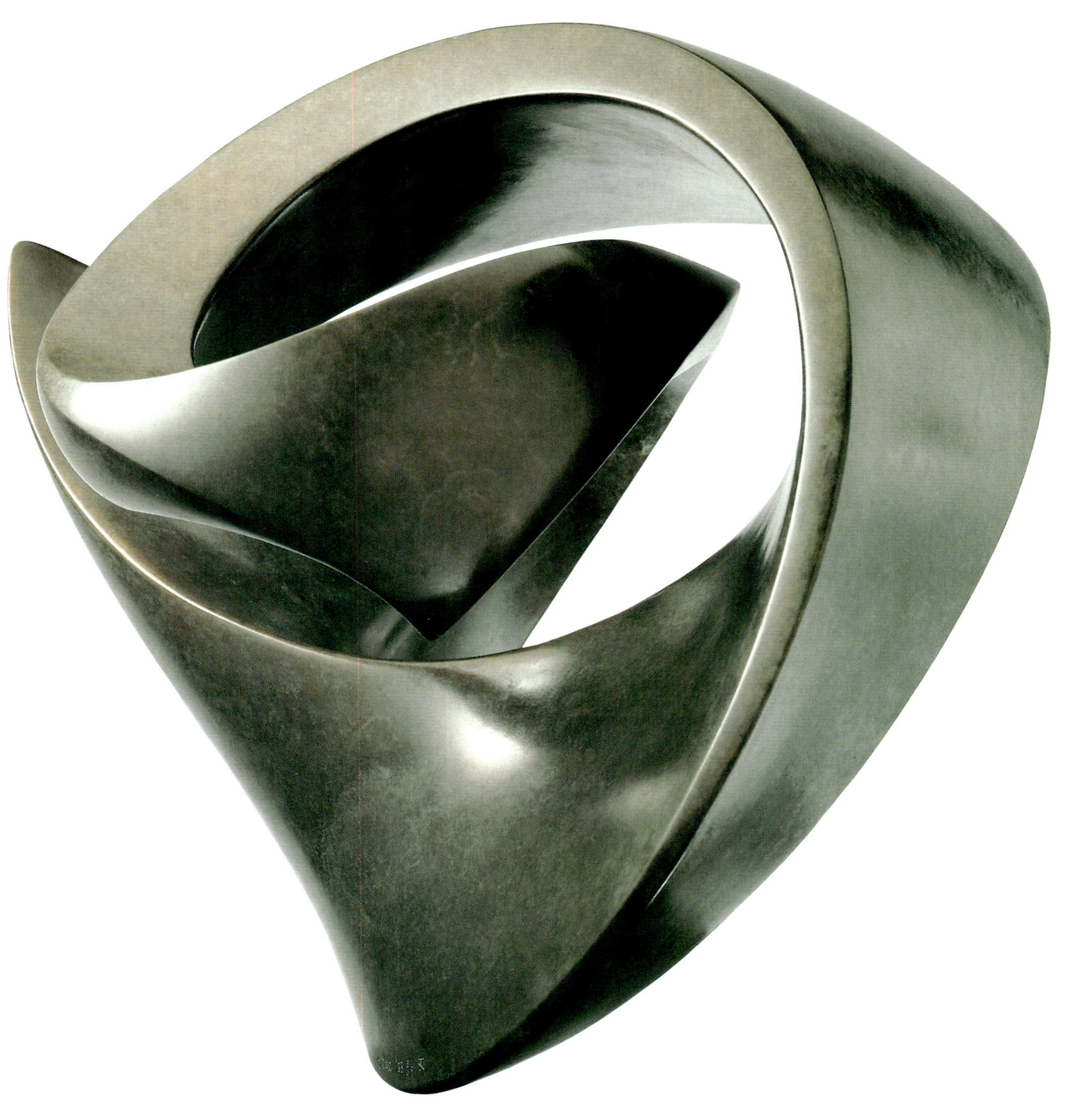

2. SINFONIETTA
Patinated bronze

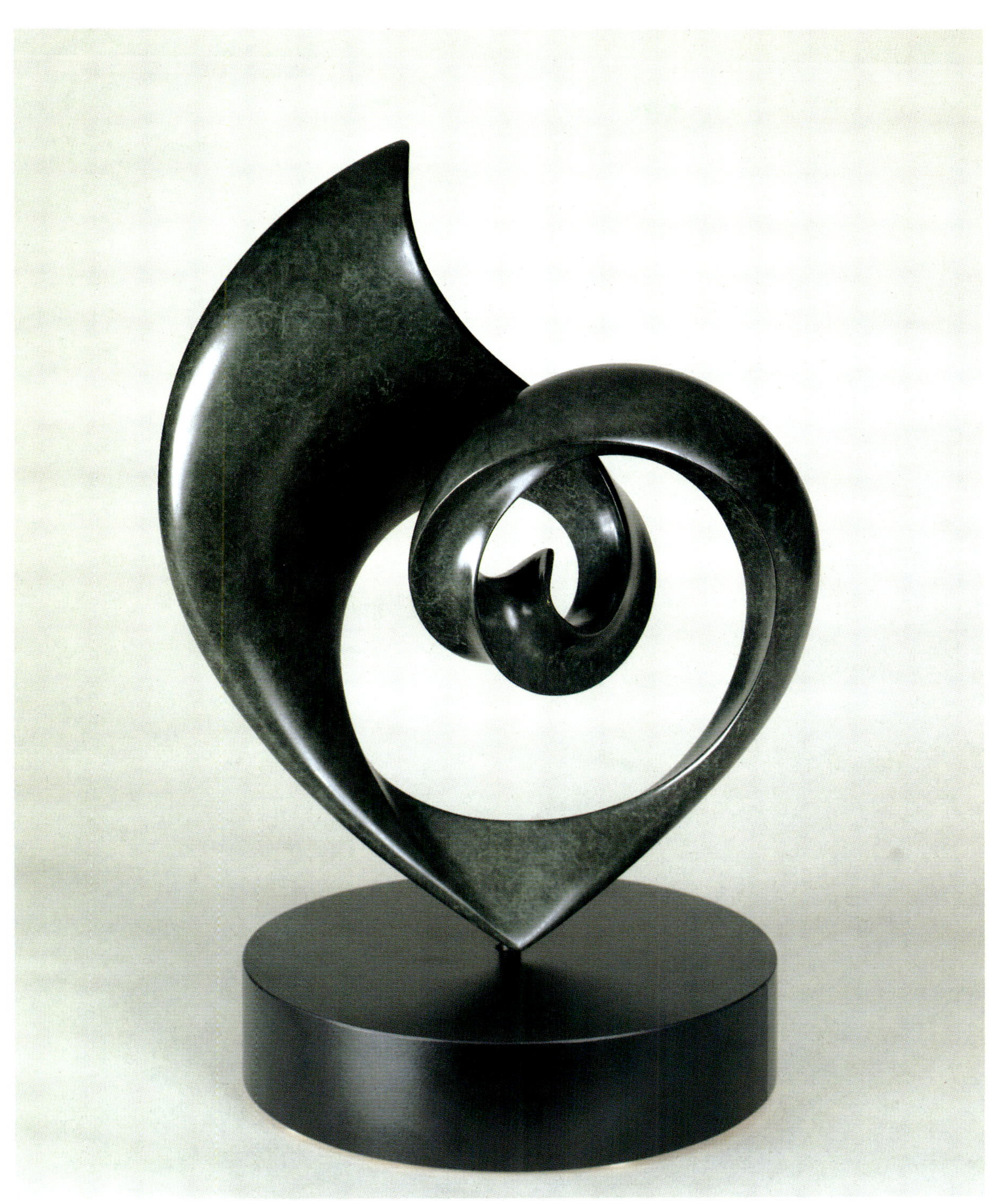

3. A UNE PASSANTE
Patinated bronze

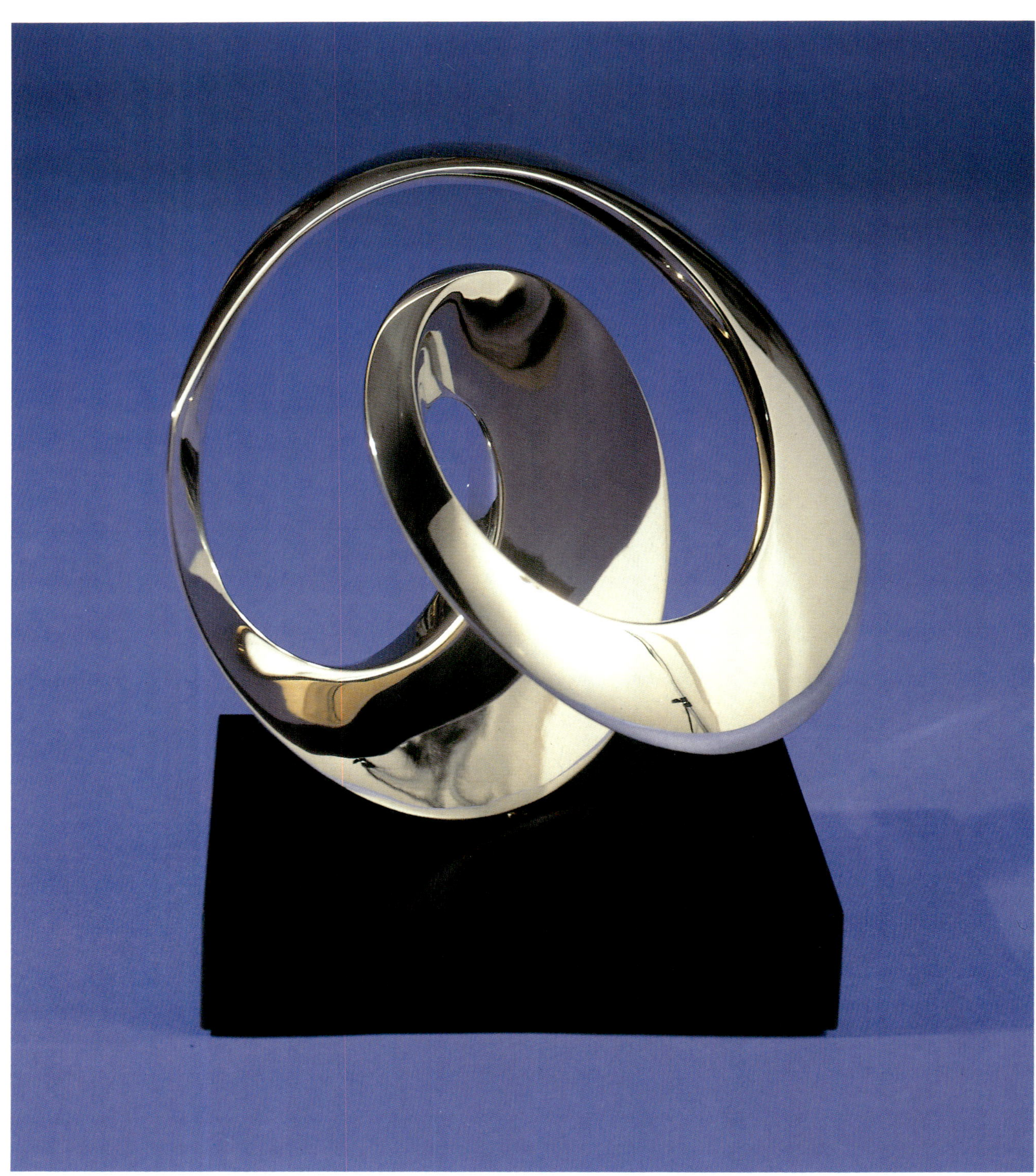

4. A CAPPELLA
Polished bronze

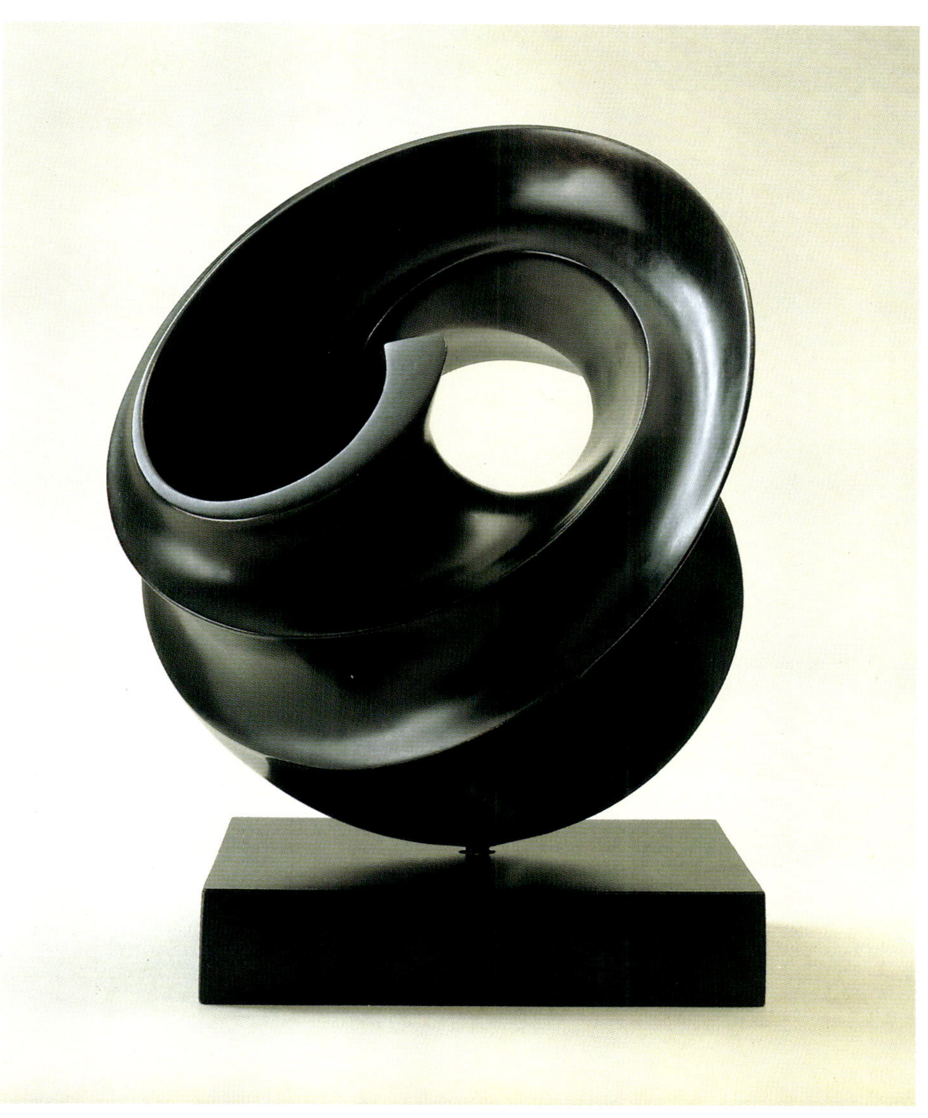

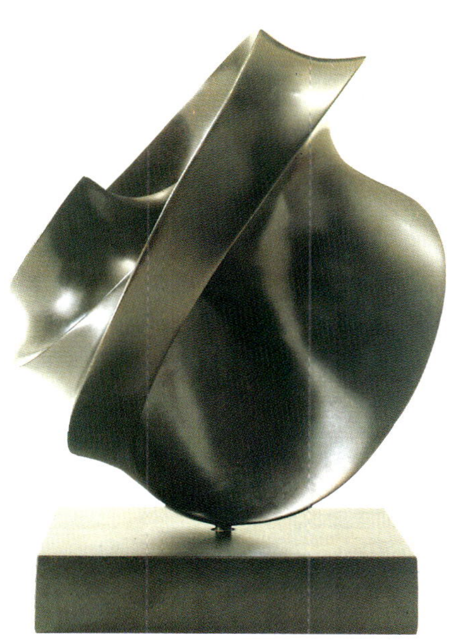

5. CONCERTO FOR WOODWIND
Patinated bronze

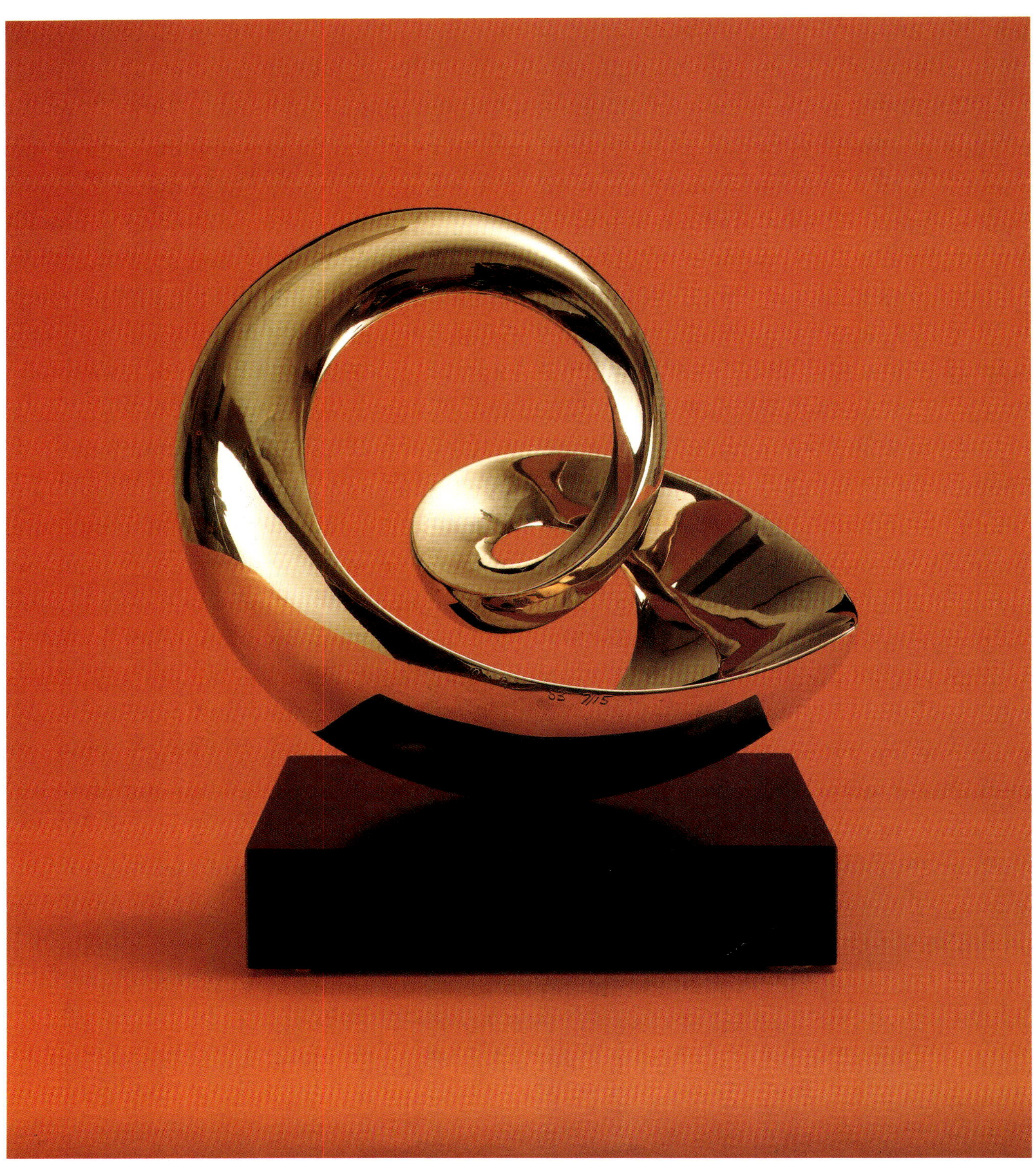

6. MAZURKA
Polished bronze

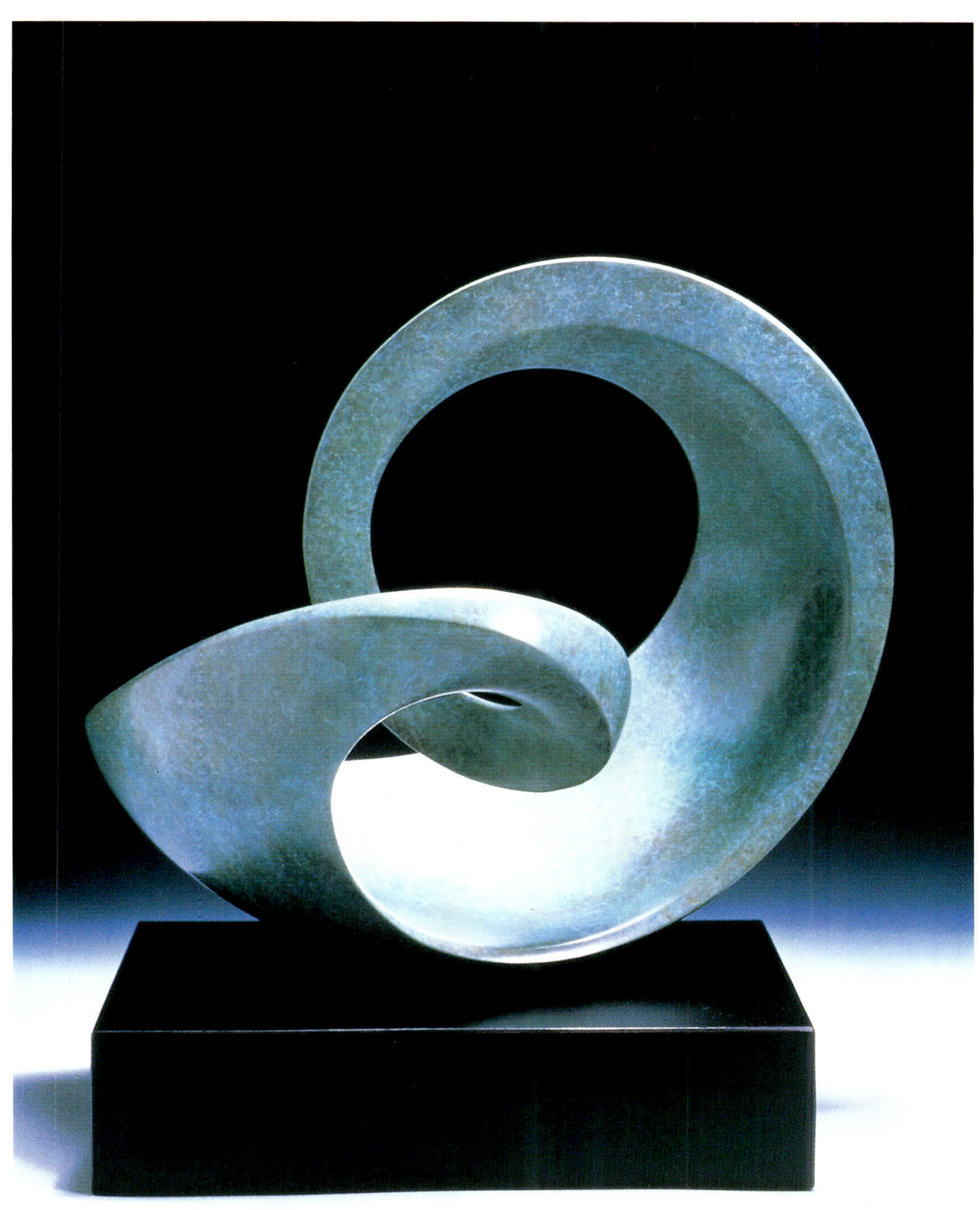

7. MAZURKA
Patinated bronze

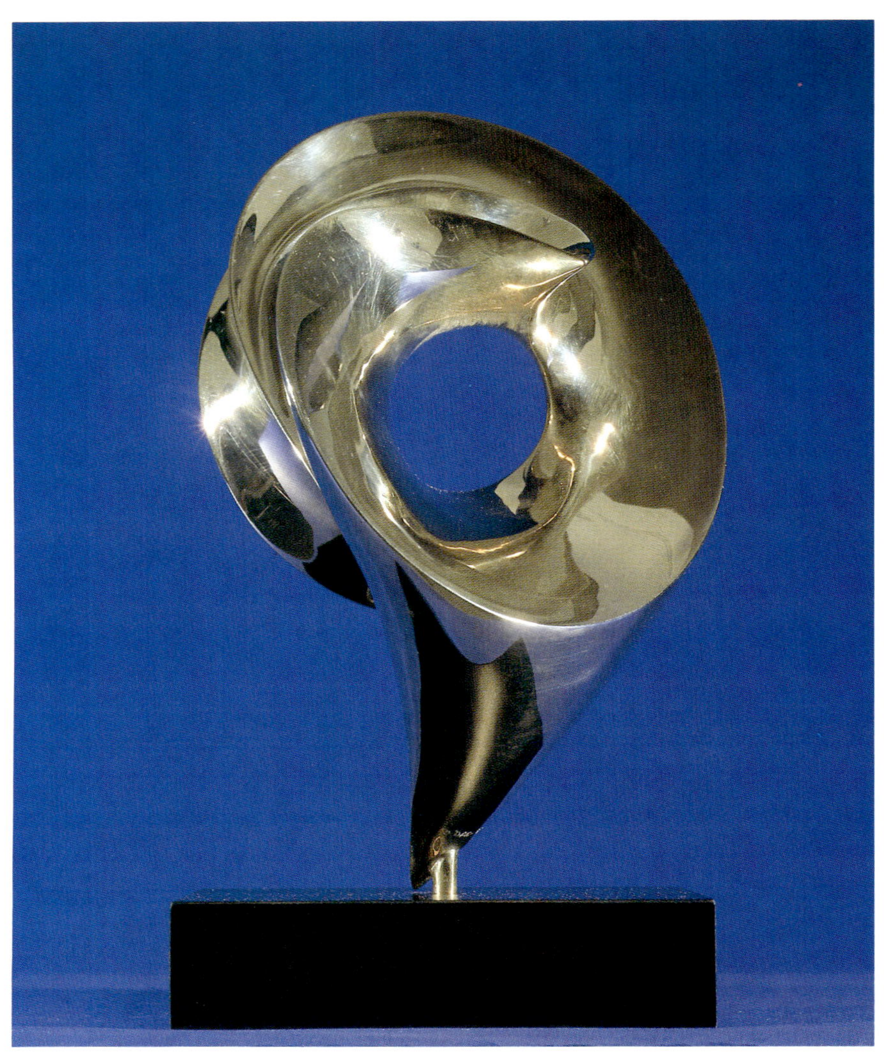

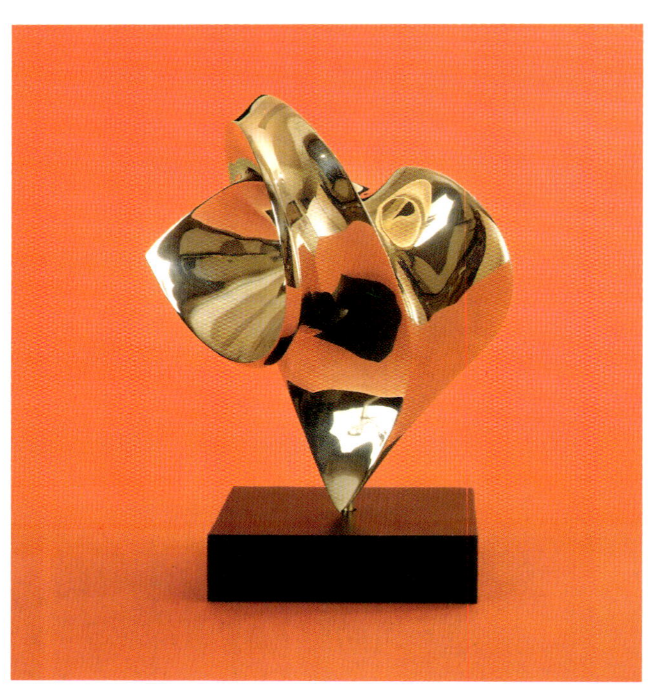

8. CONCERTO FOR BRASS
Polished bronze

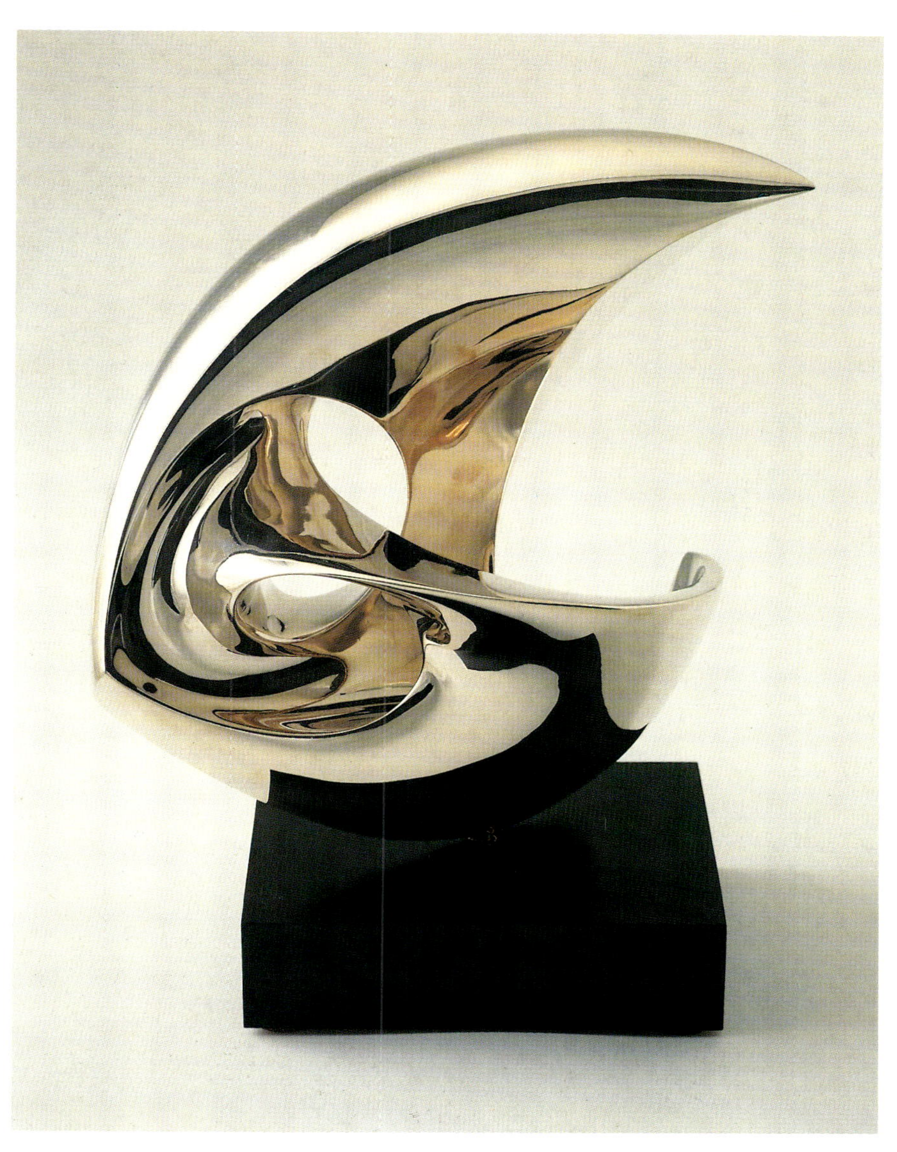

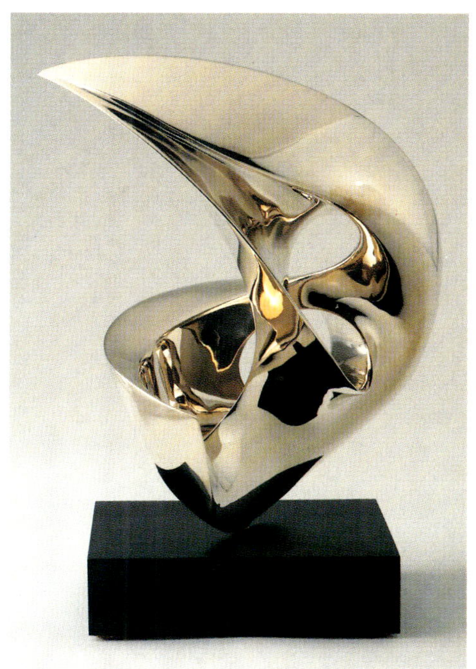

9. FESTIVALE
Polished bronze

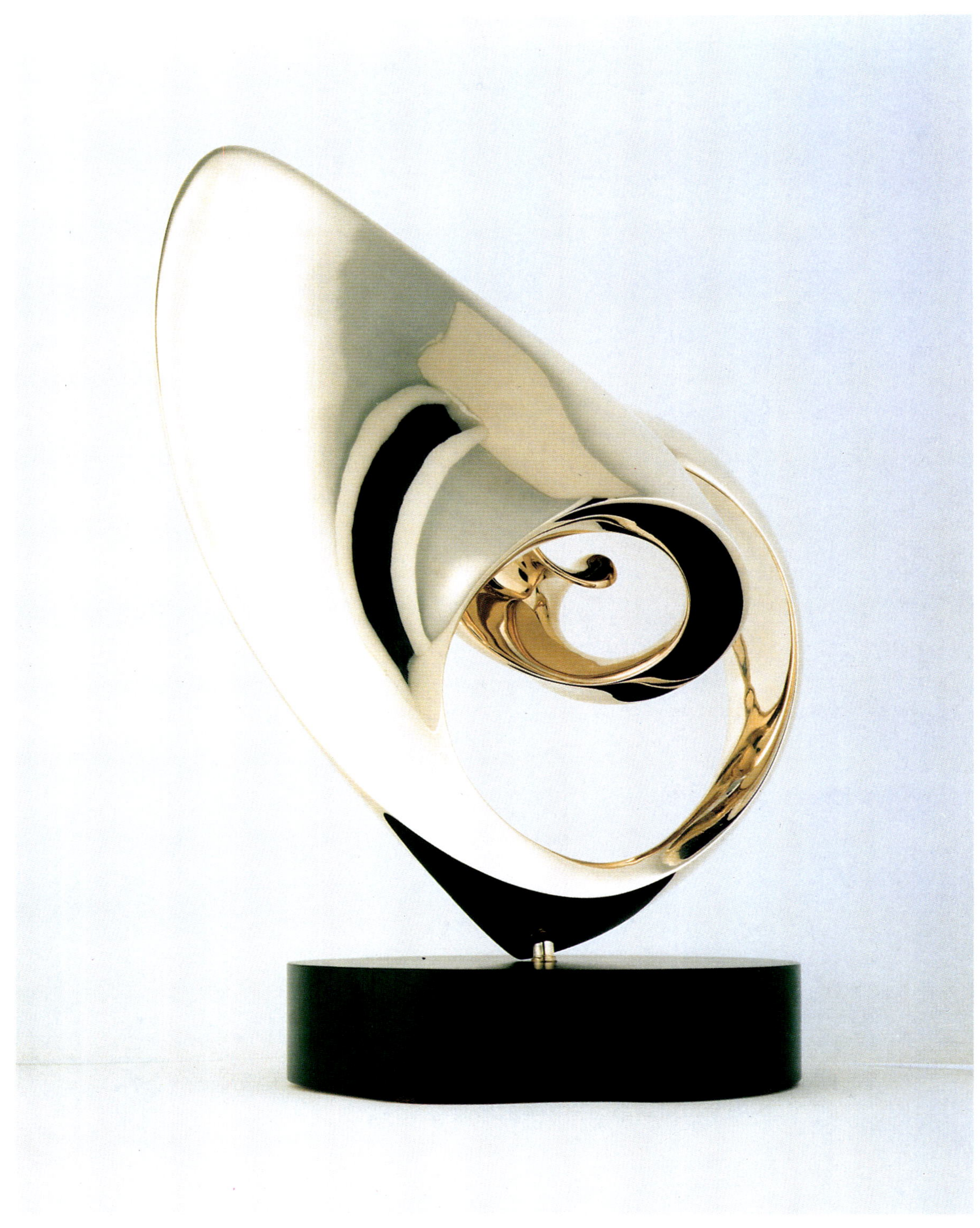

10. HEARTSONG
Polished bronze

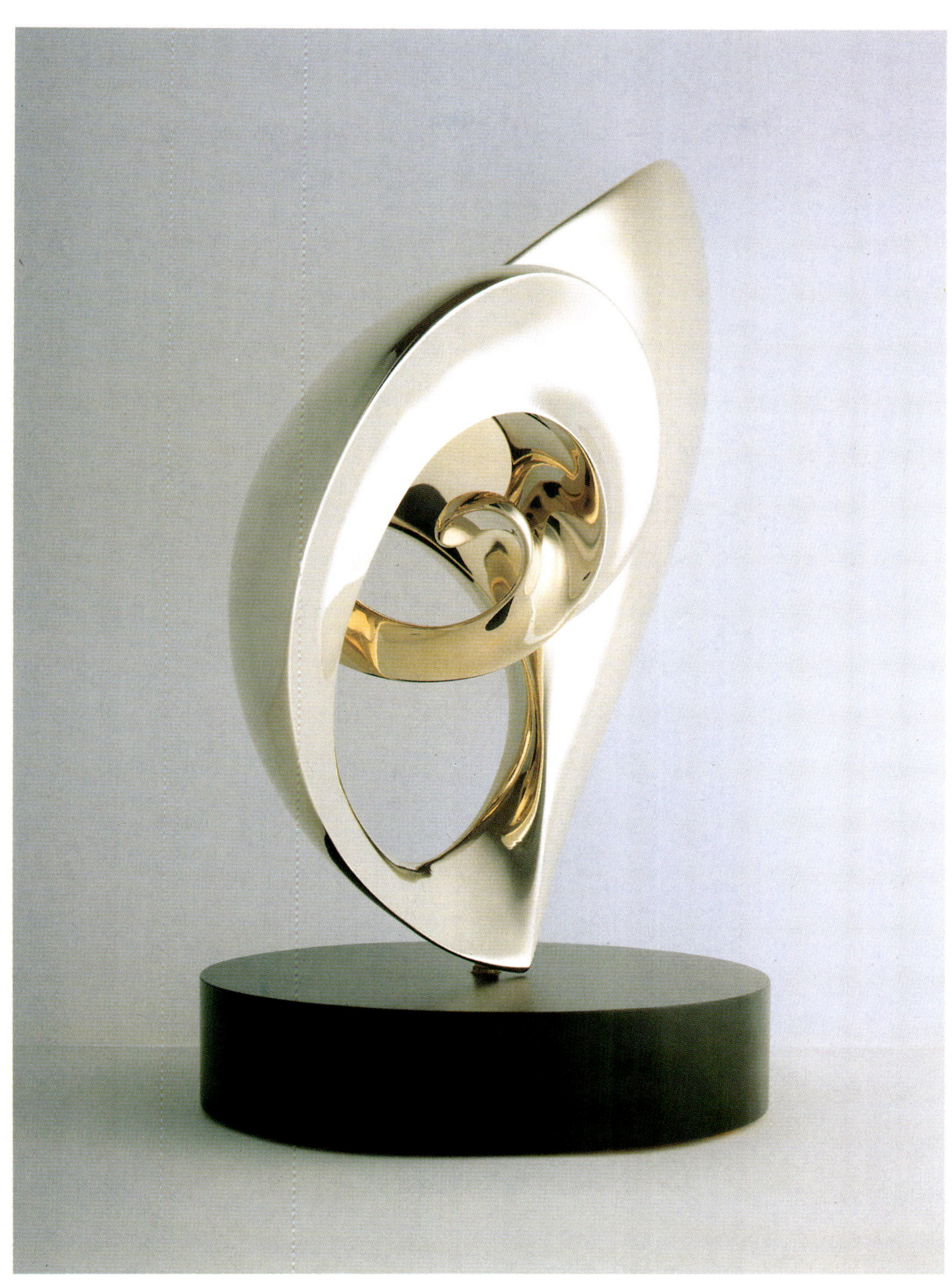

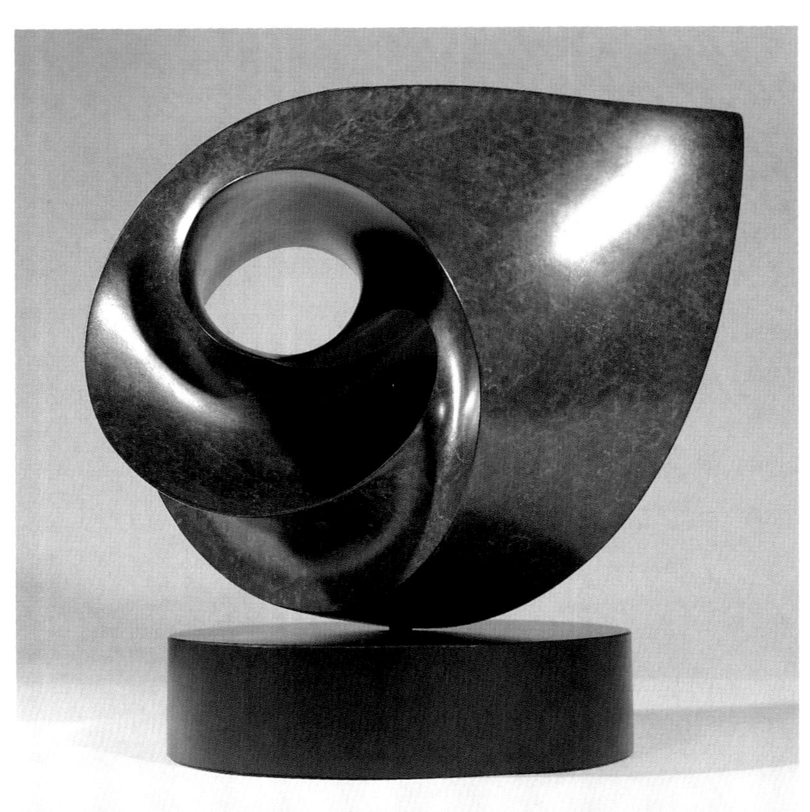

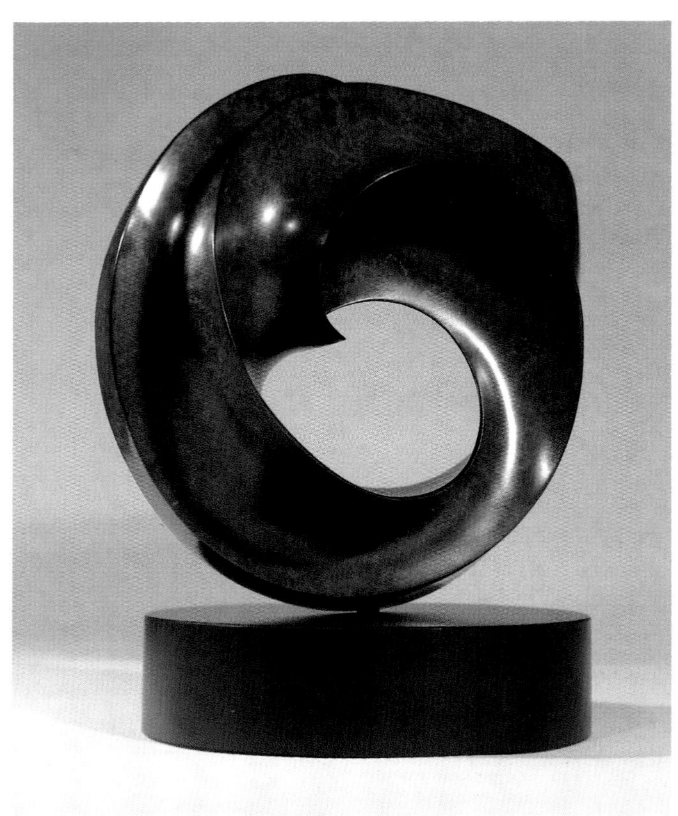

11. PARFUMS DE LA NUIT
Patinated bronze

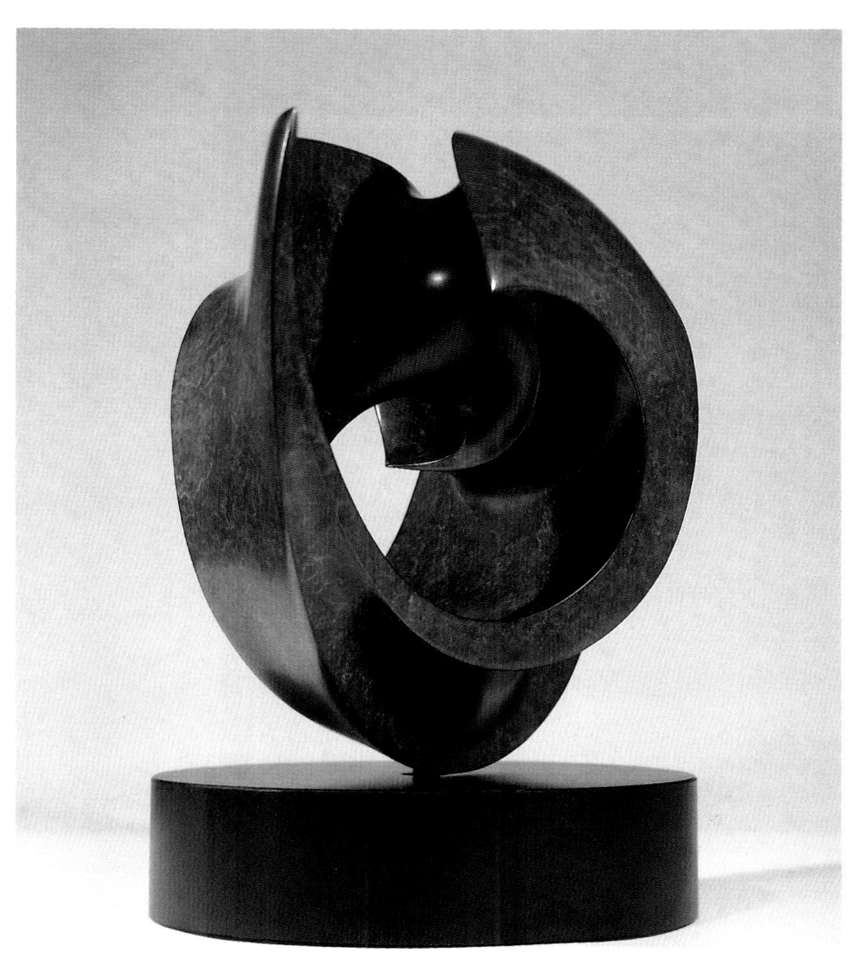

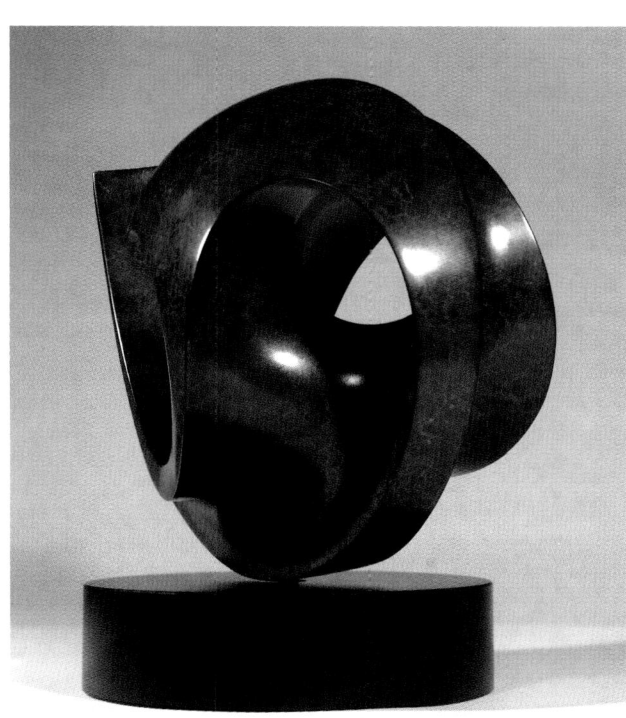

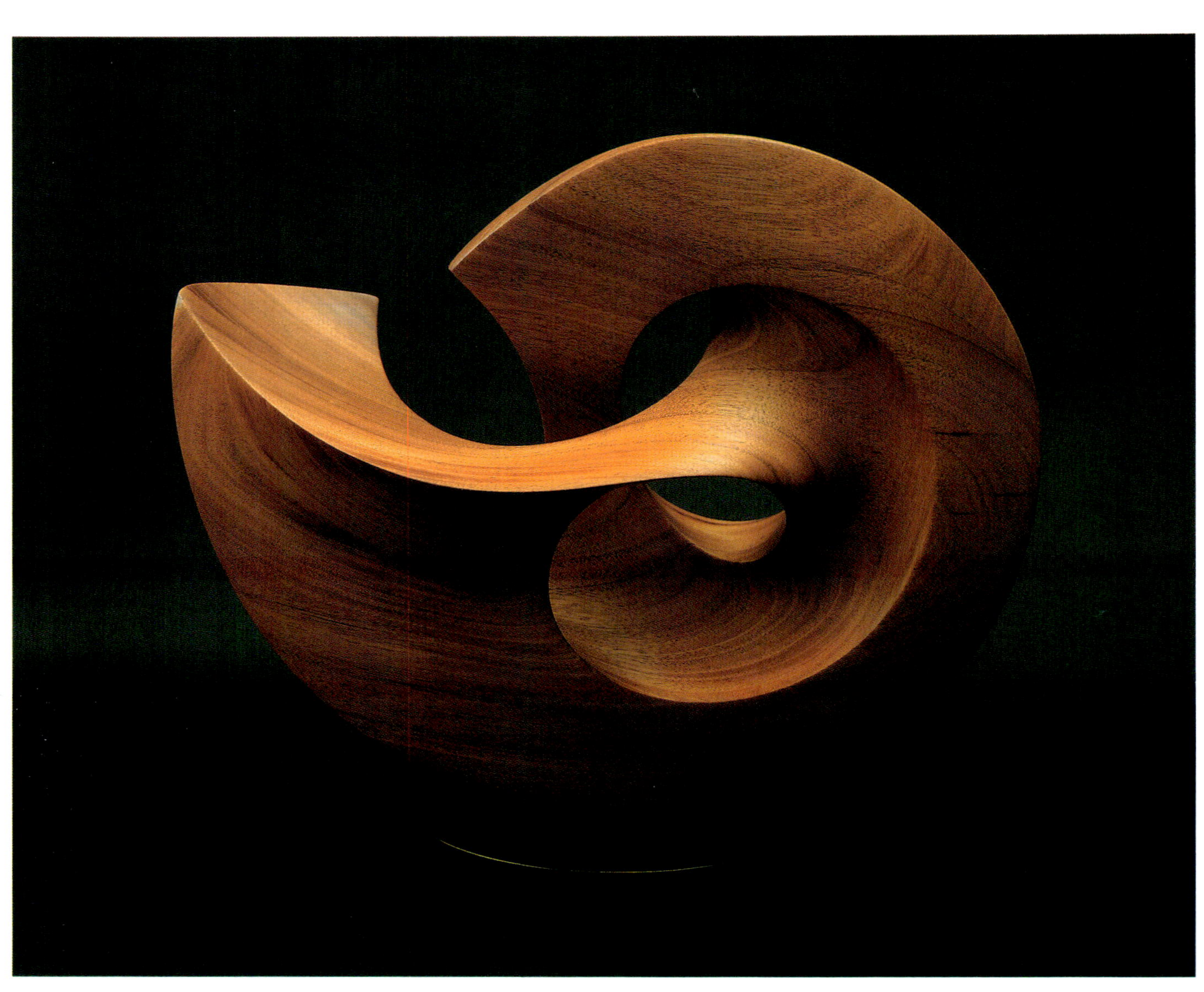

12. SCHEHEREZADE
Mahogany

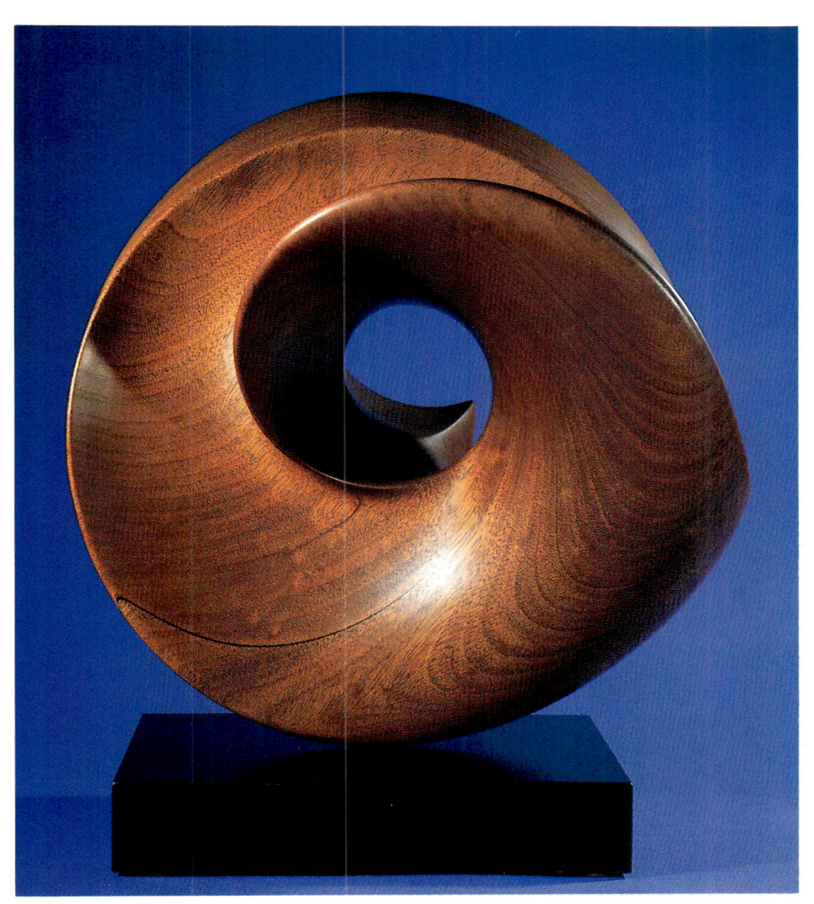

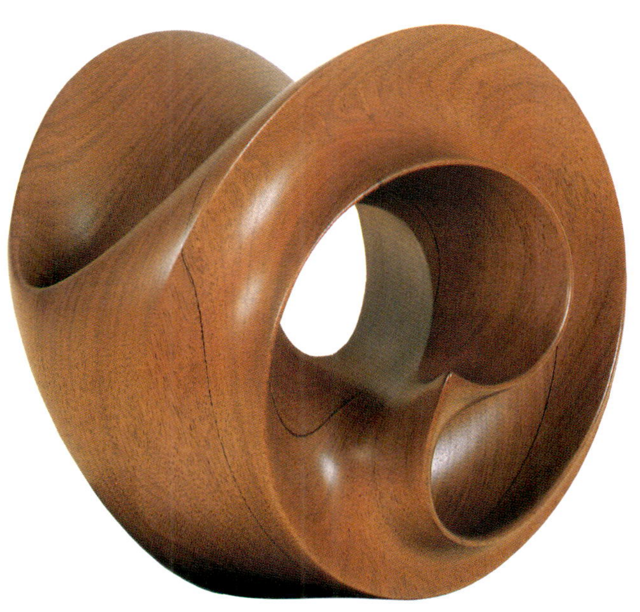

13. ENIGMATIC VARIATION #9
Mahogany

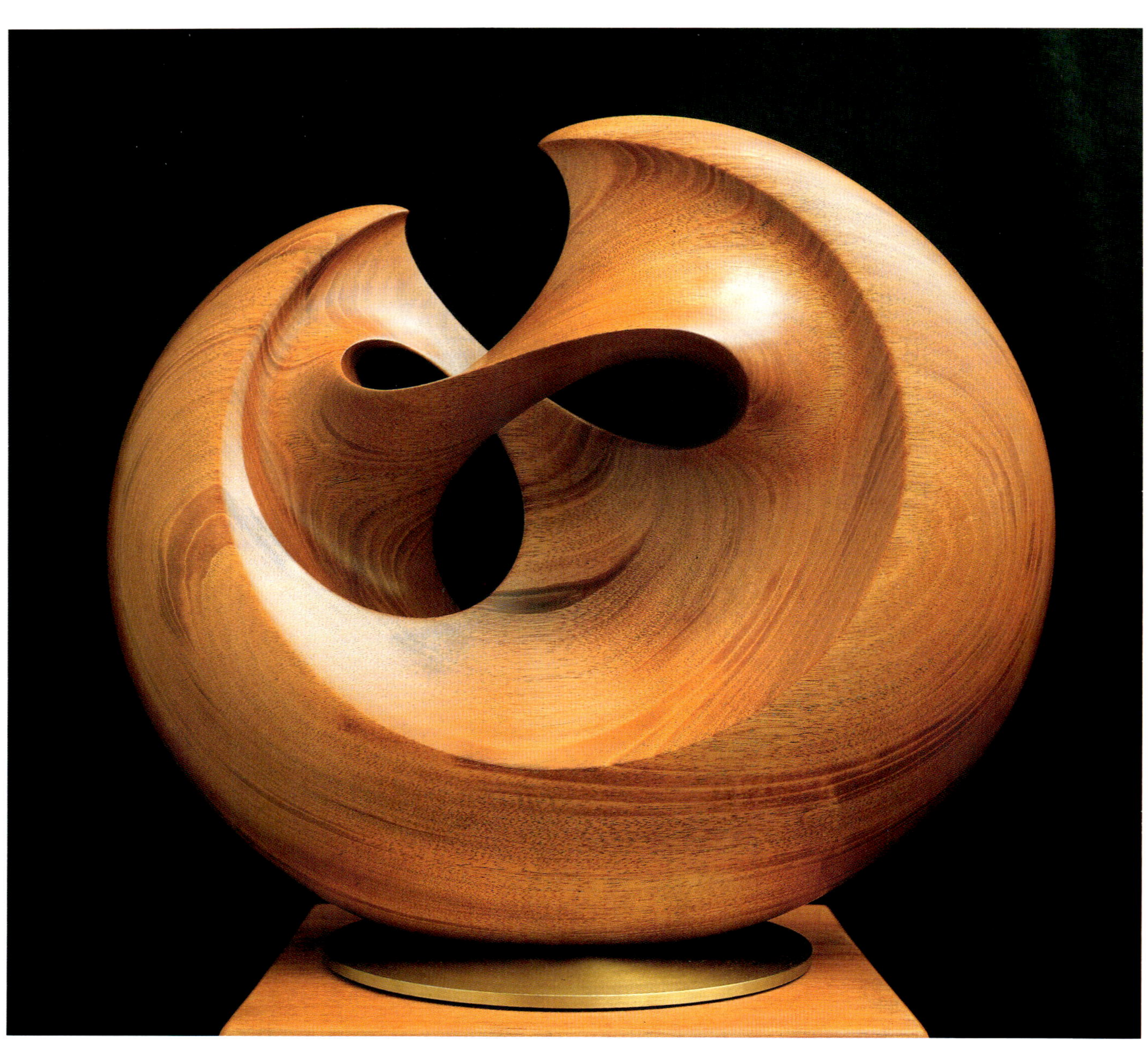

14. AKIMBO
Mahogany

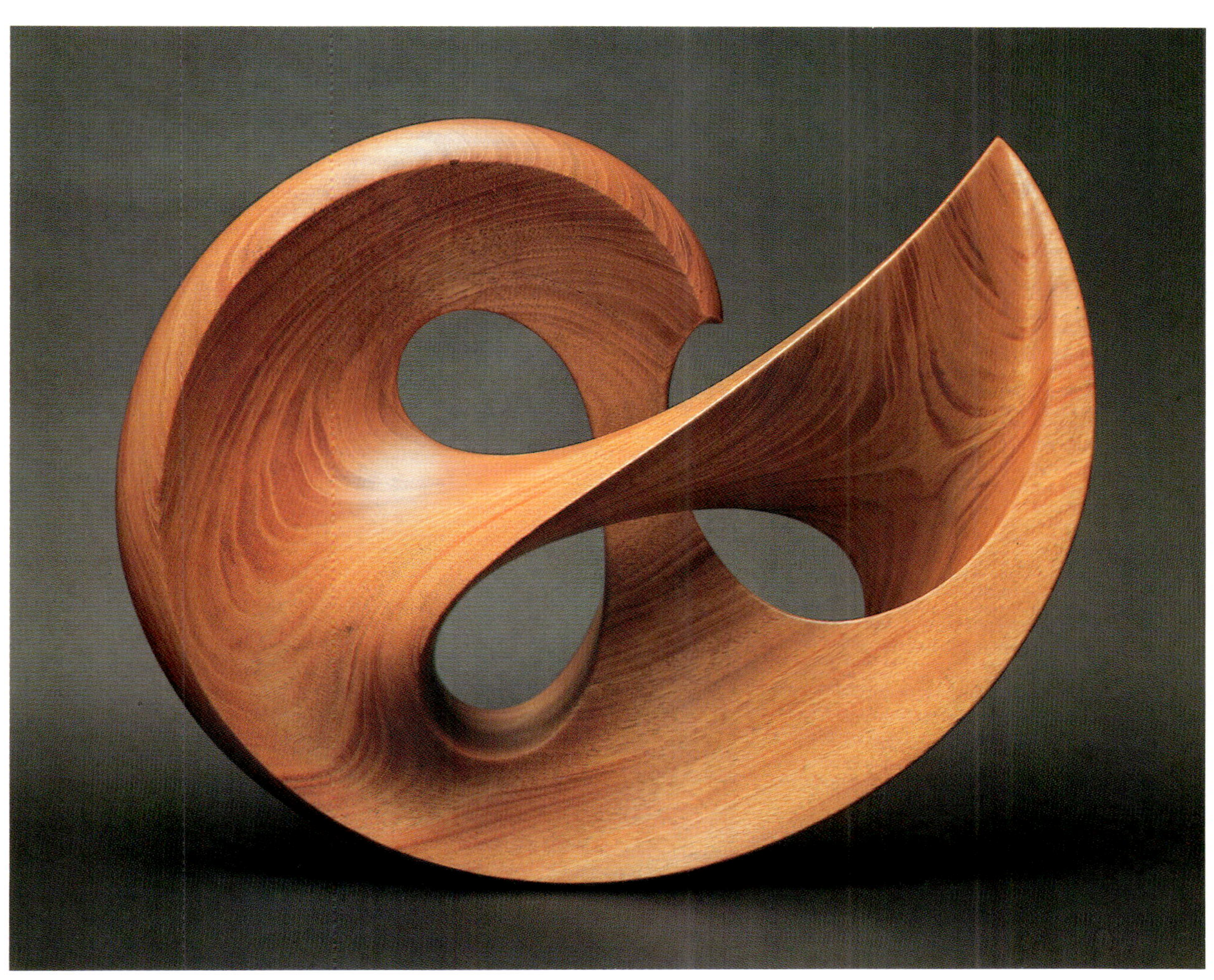

15. ADAGIO
Mahogany

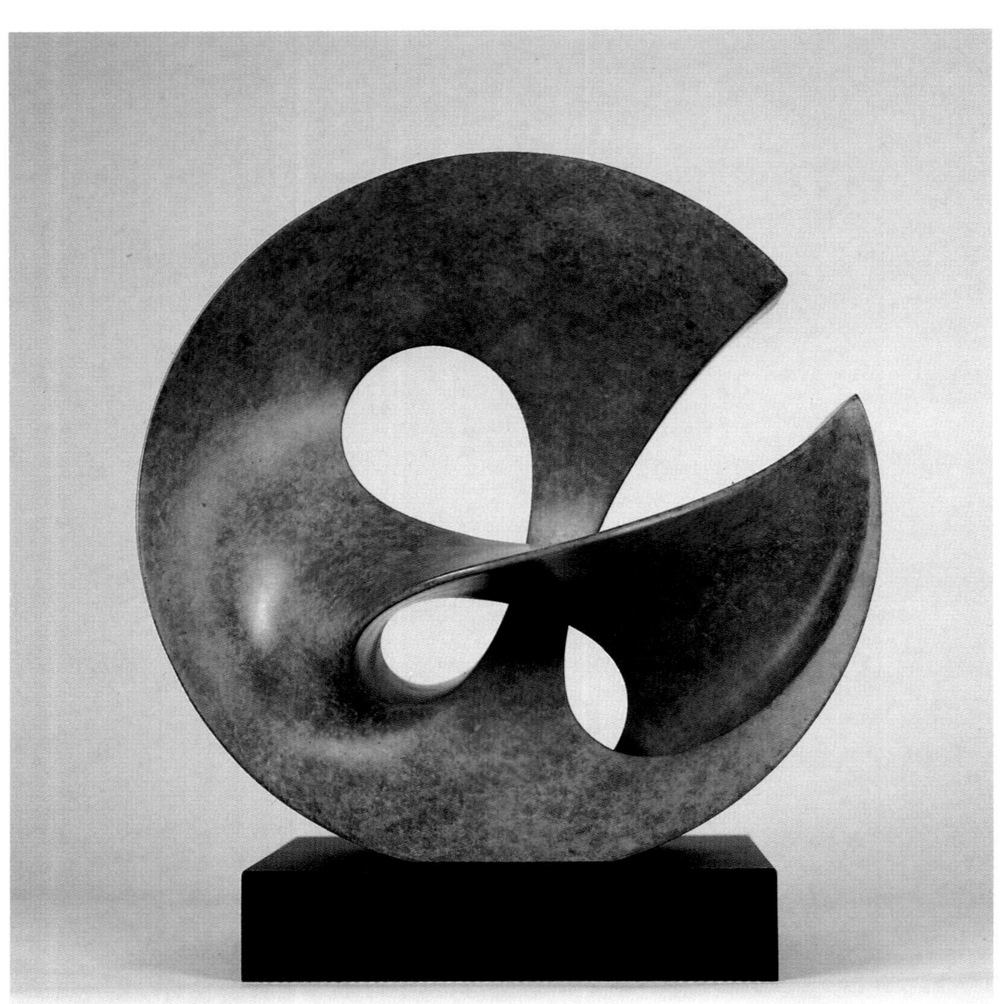

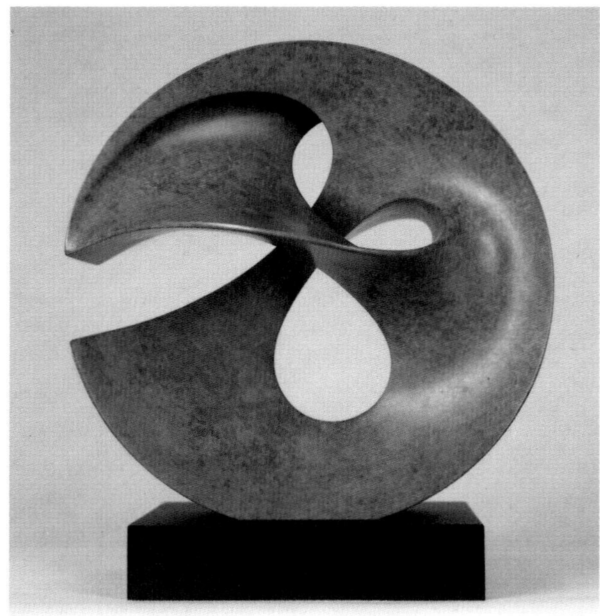

16. OPEN CLEFF
Patinated bronze

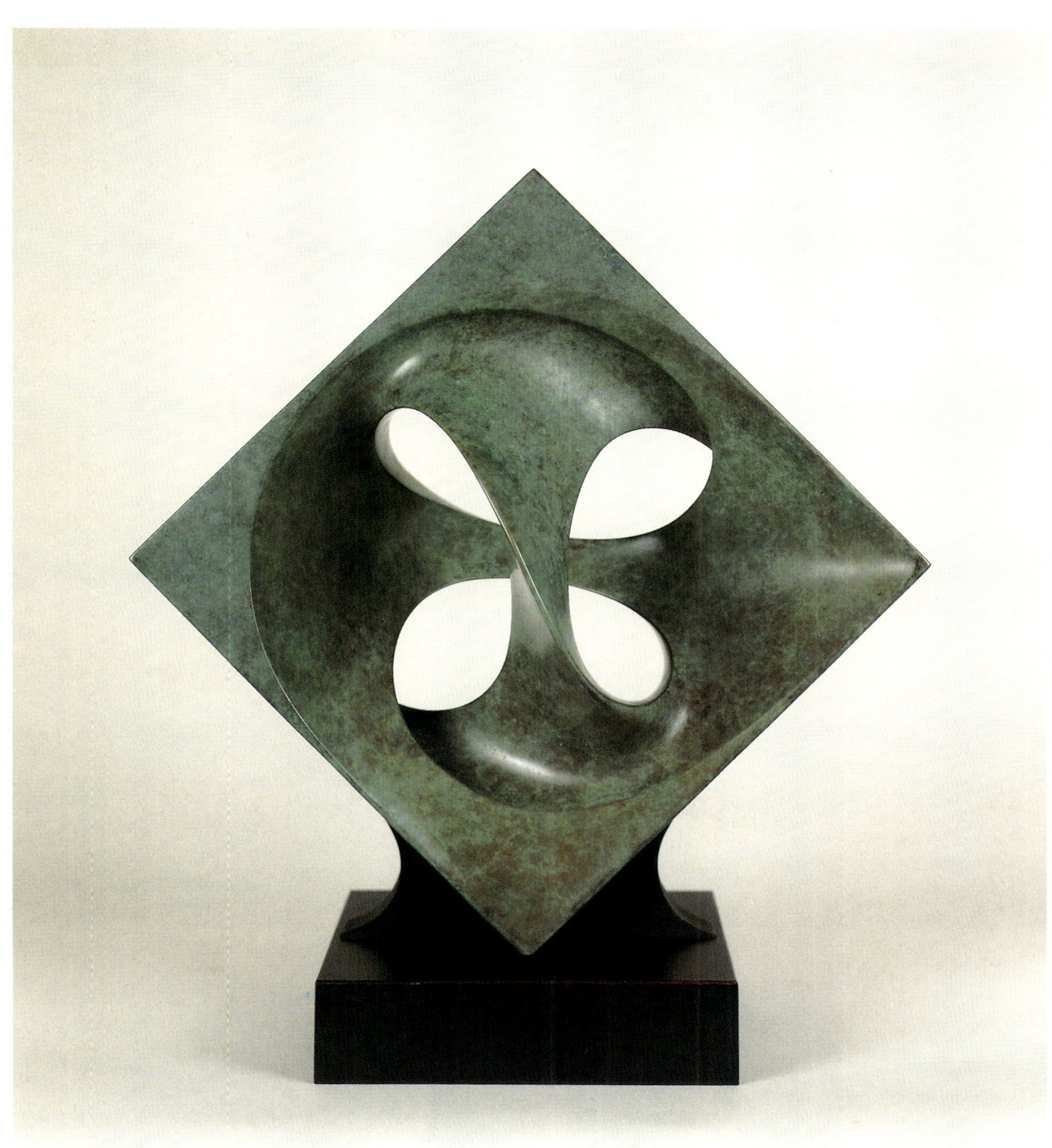

17. QUARTETTA
Patinated bronze

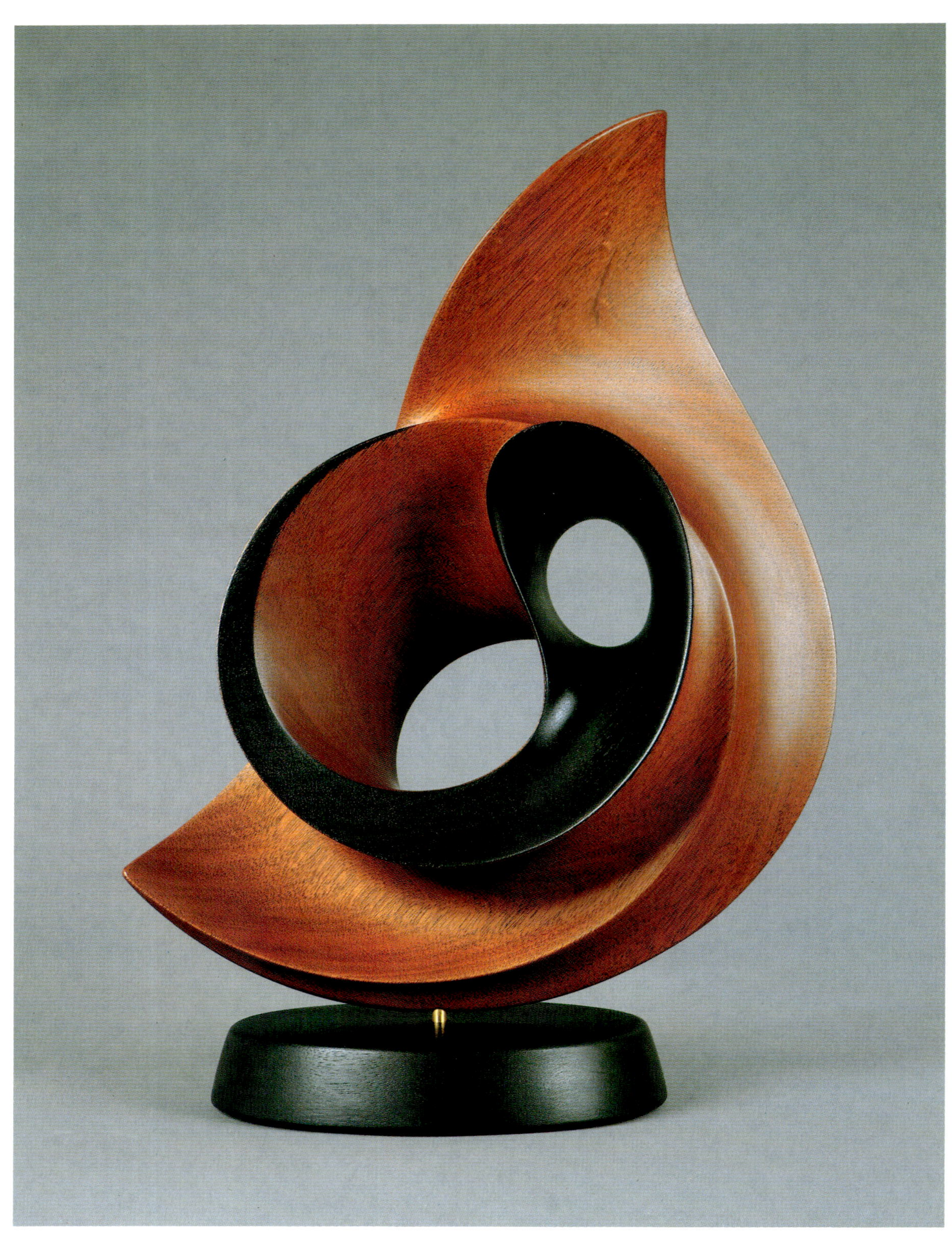

18. POISSON D'OR #15
Mahogany polychrome

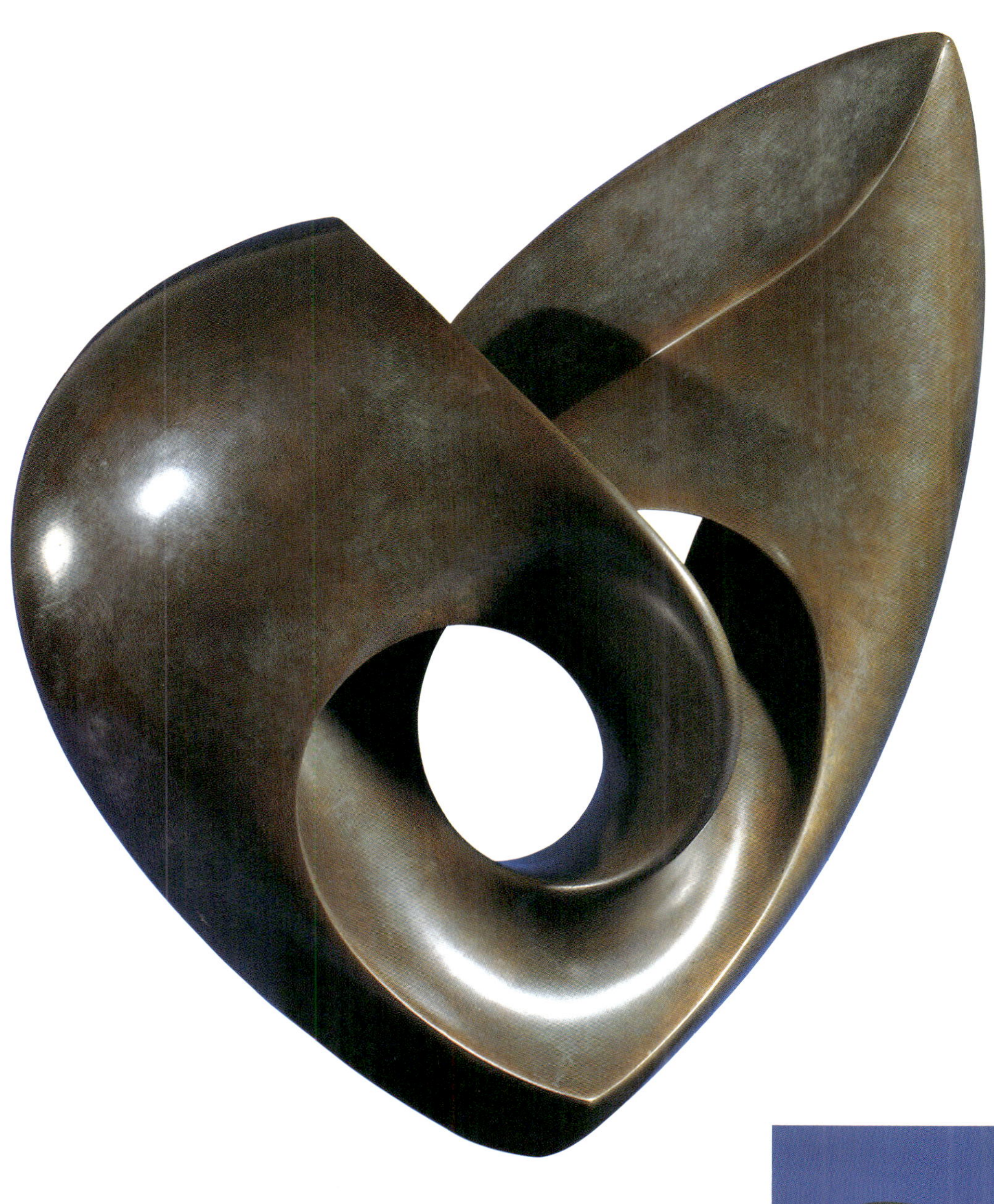

19. RHAPSODY
Patinated bronze

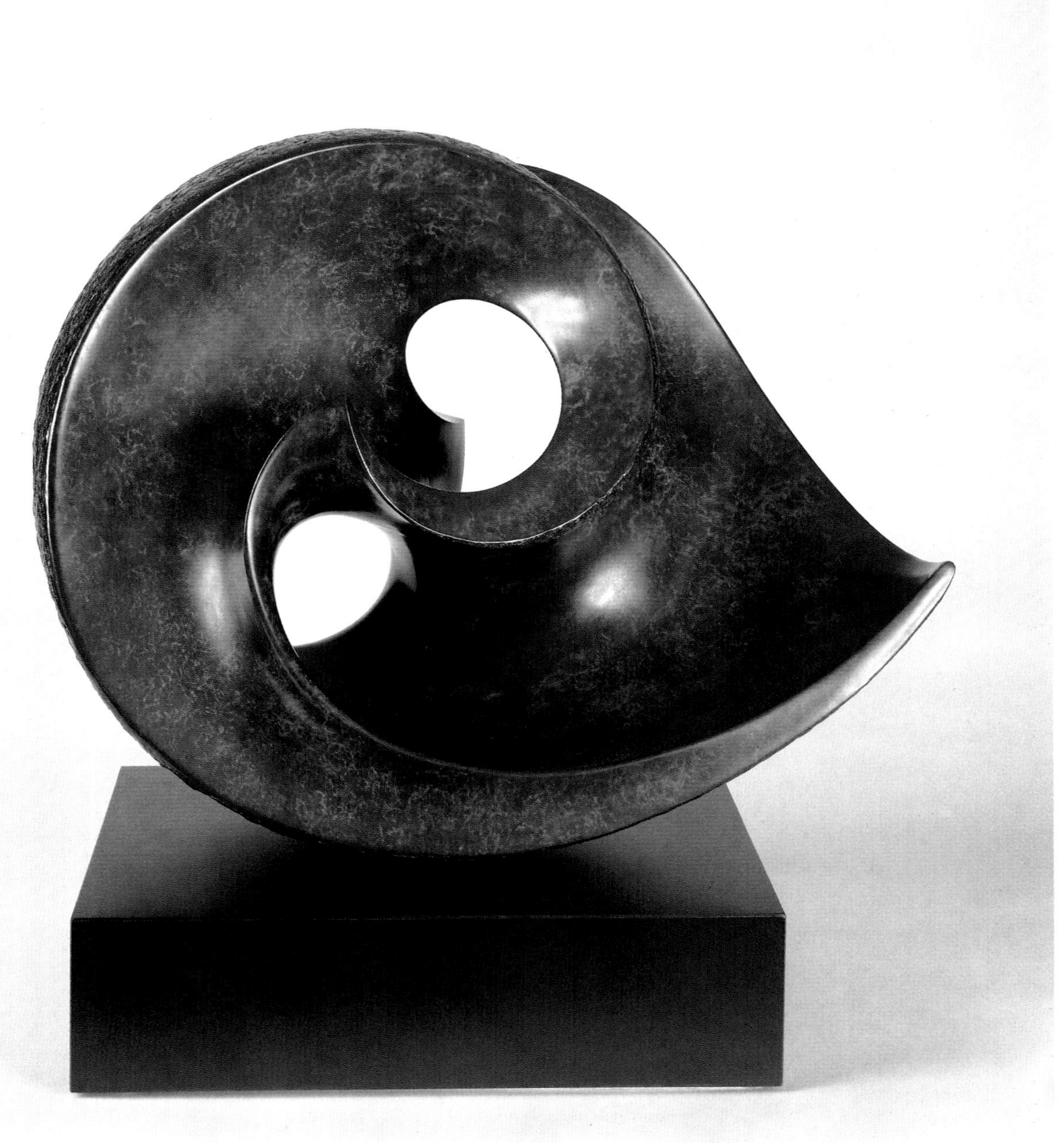

20. EMBRYONS
Patinated bronze

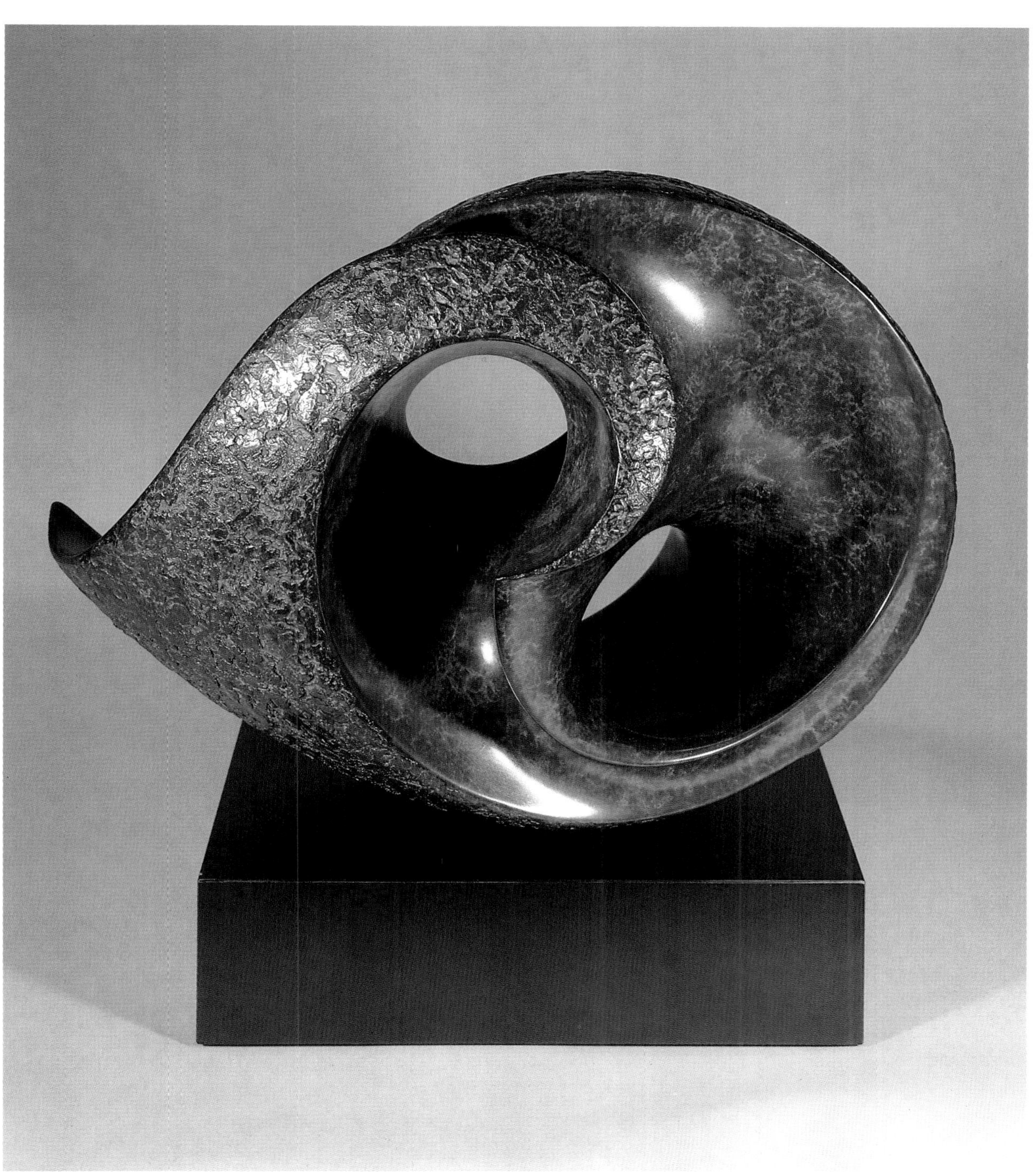

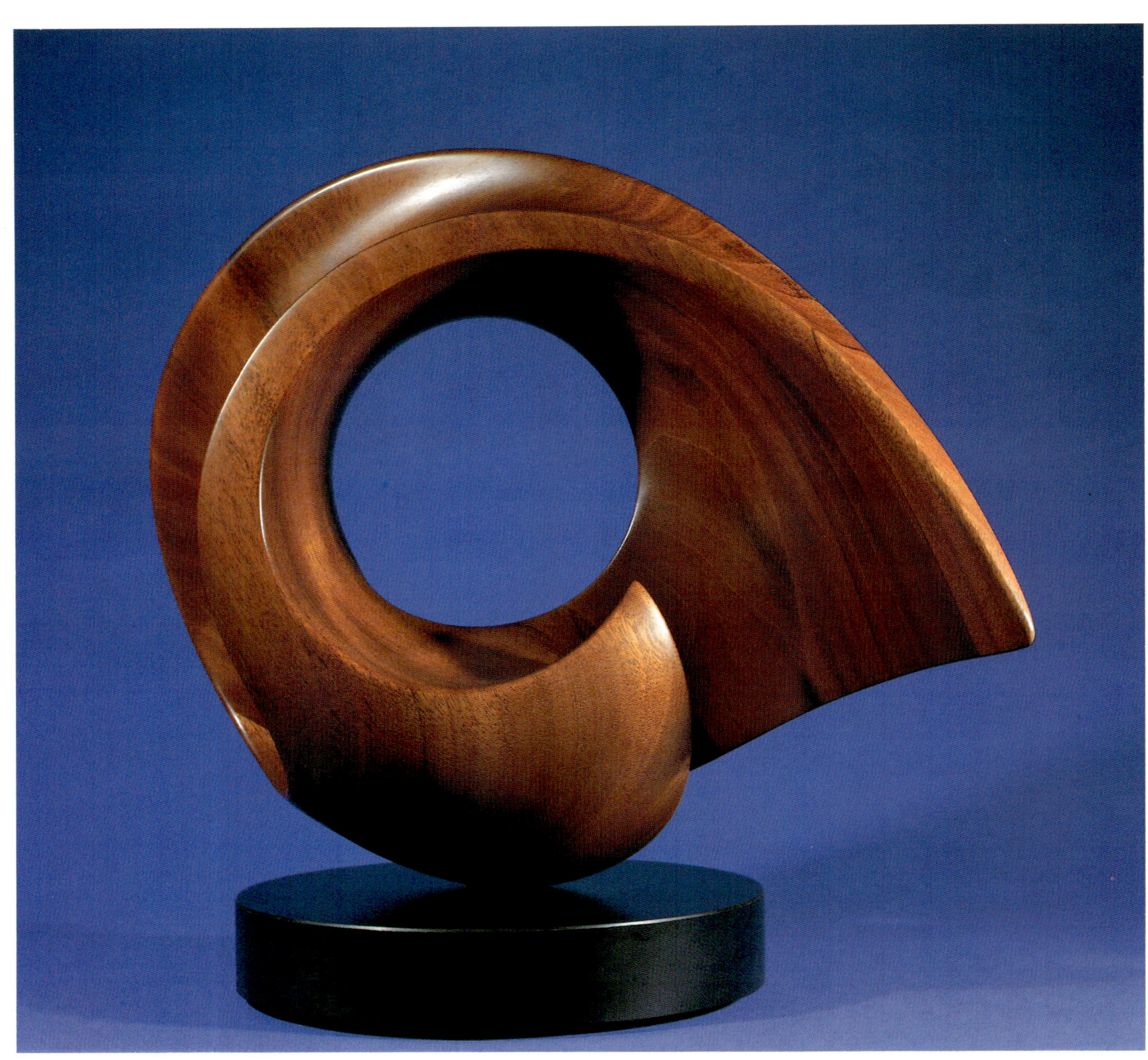

21. MOKU NO KAZE
Mahogany

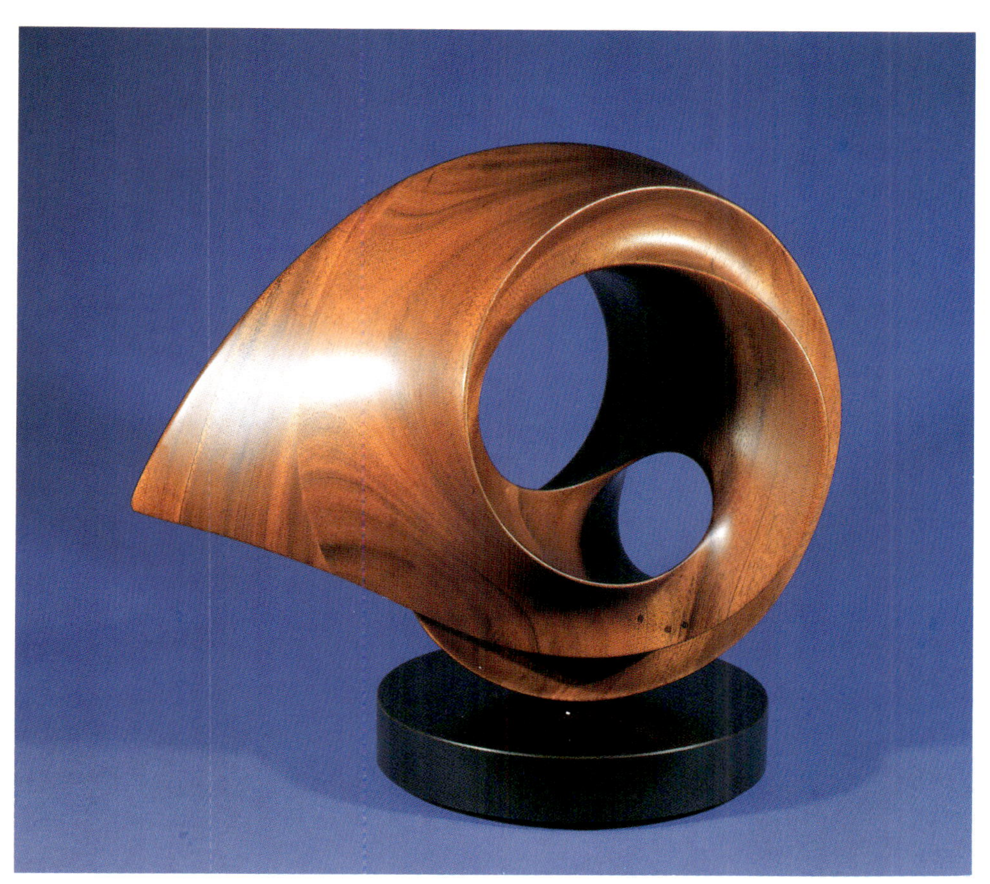

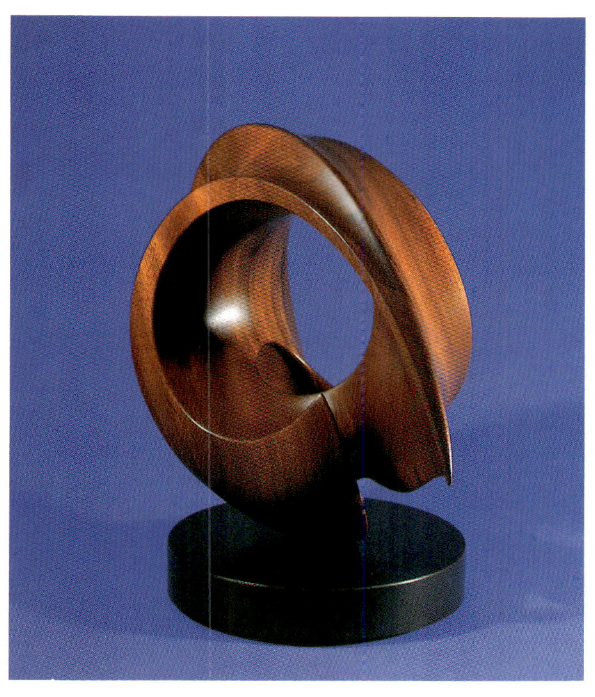

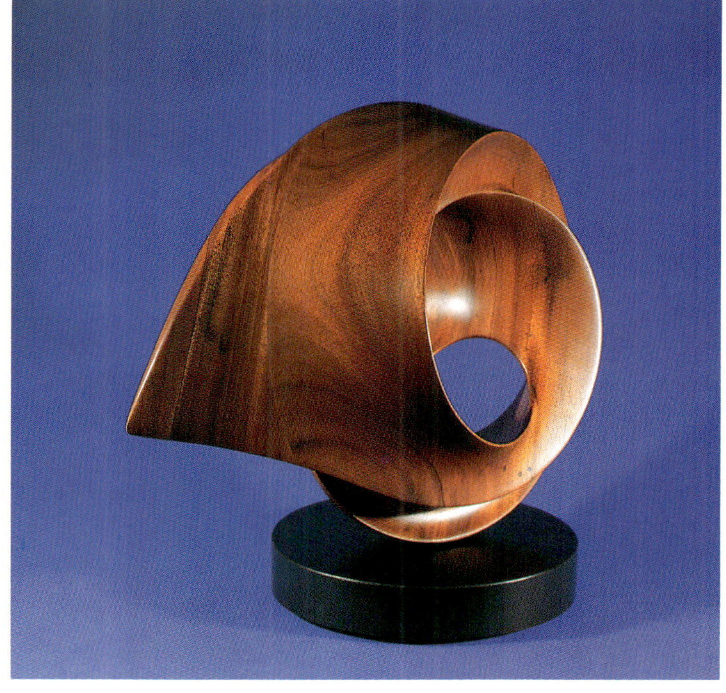

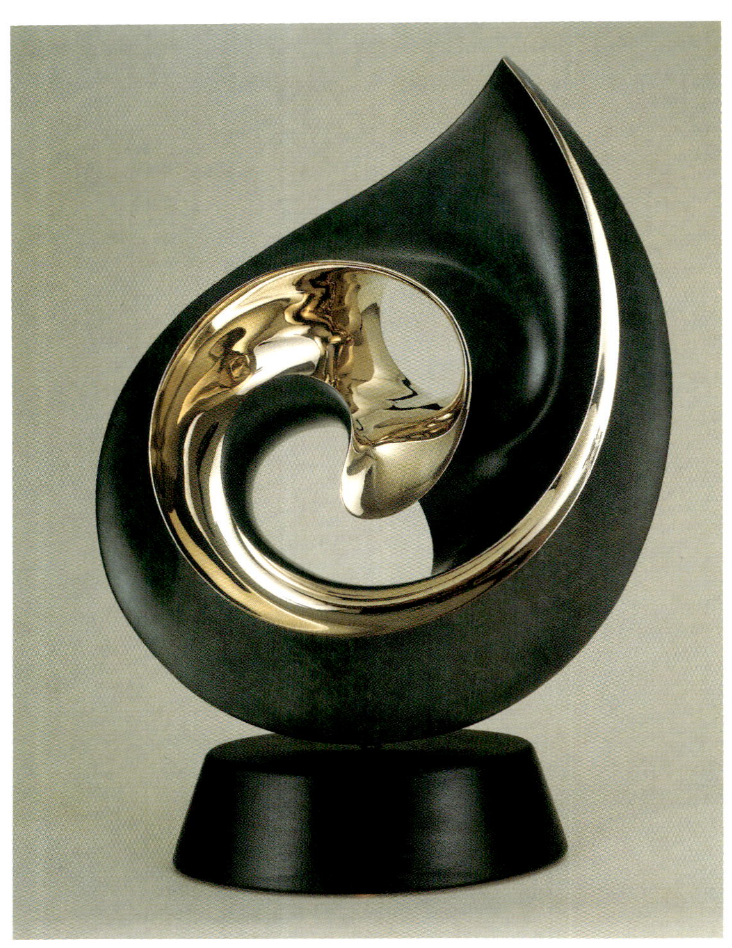

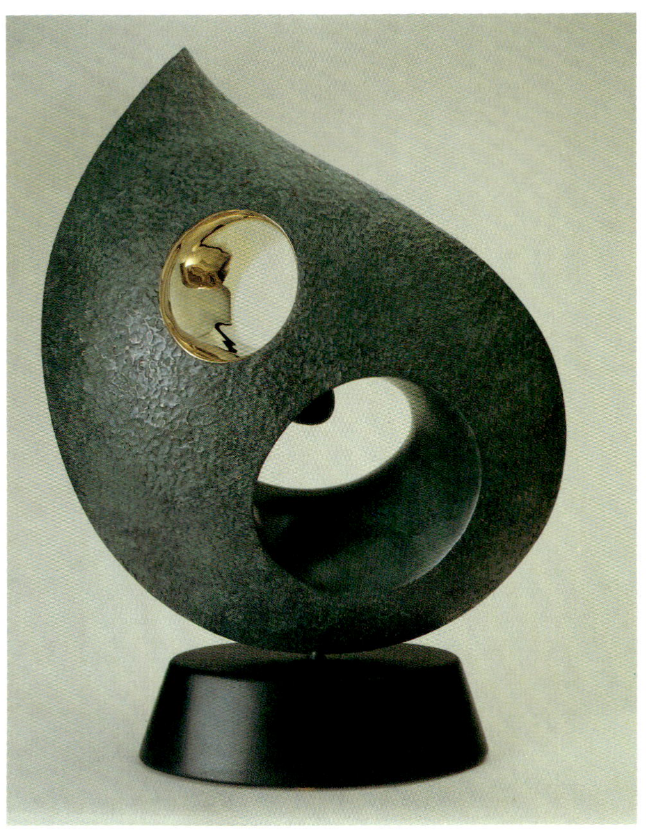

22. POISSON D'OR #10
Patinated and polished bronze

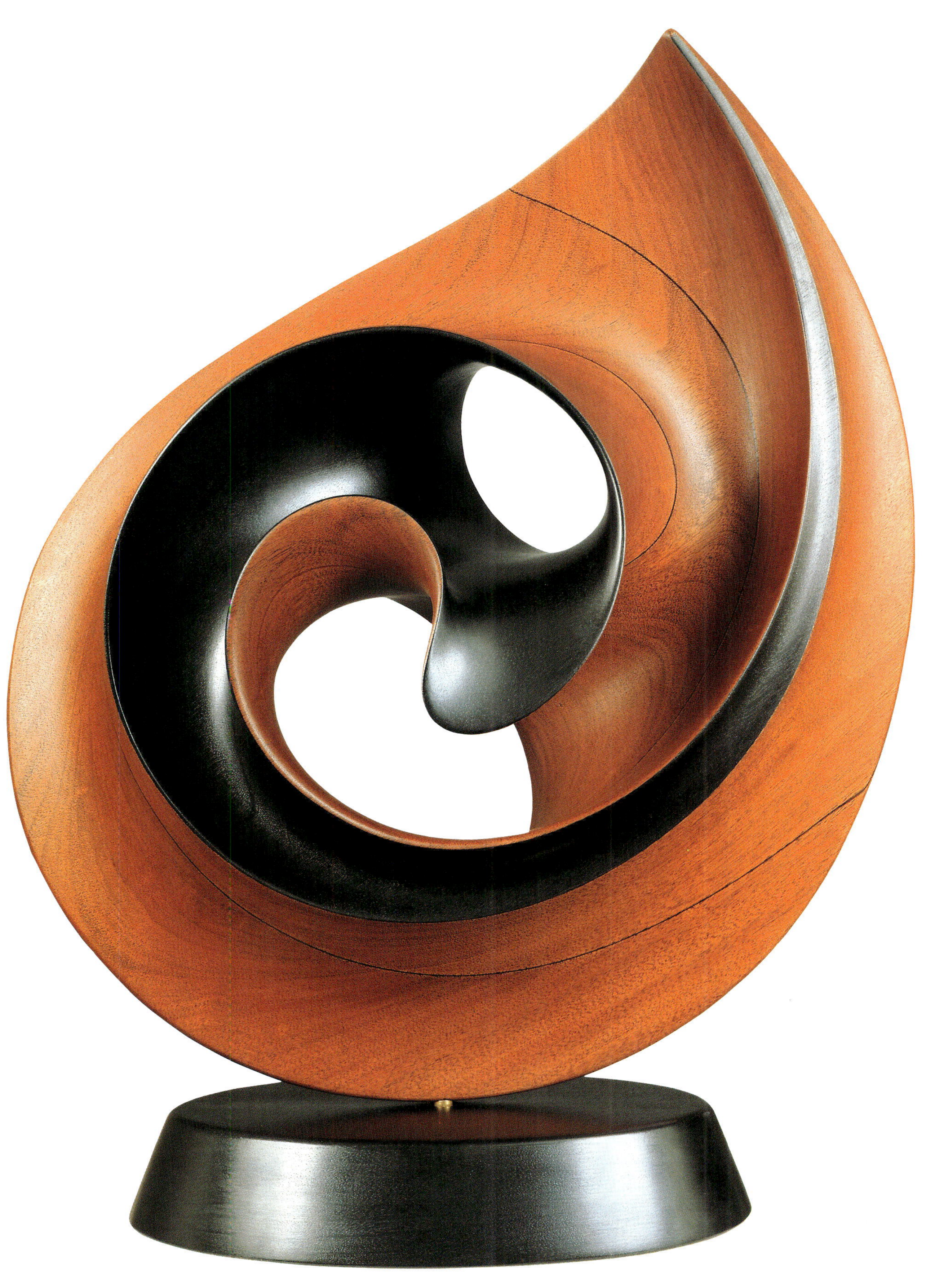

23. POISSON D'OR #10
Mahogany

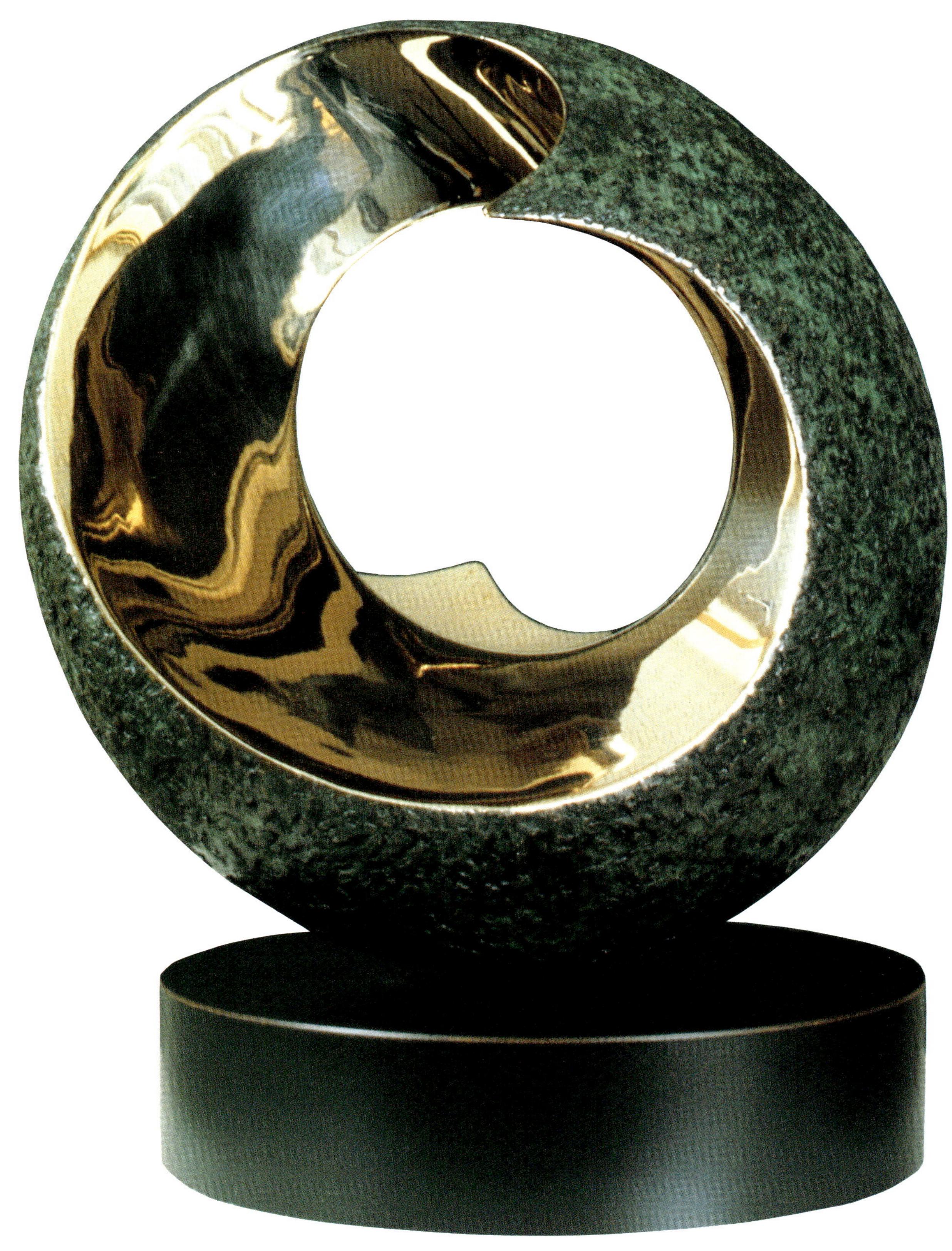

24. BALLETTA
Patinated and polished bronze

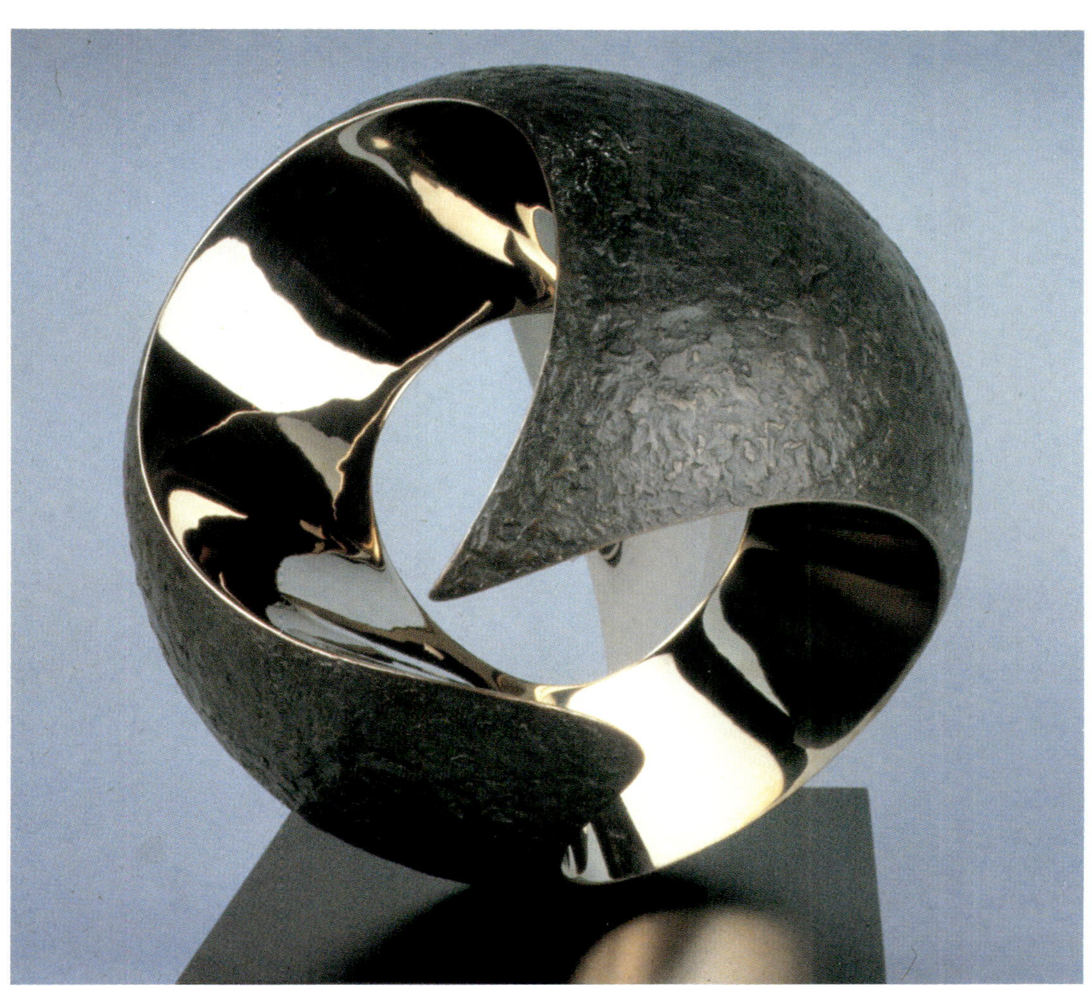

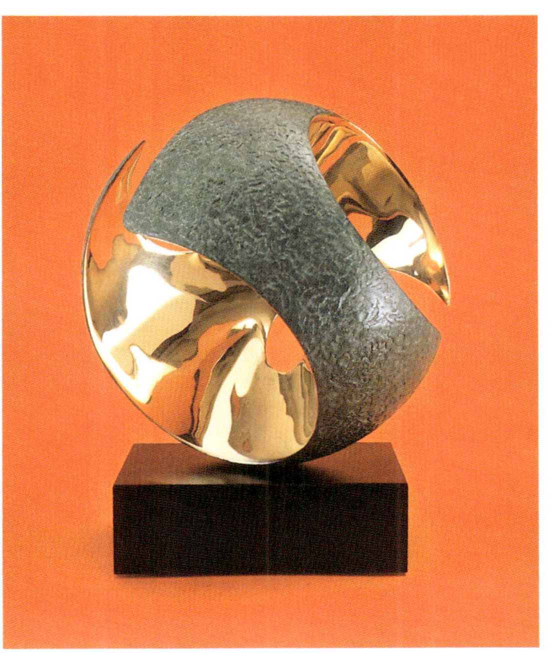

25. BALLADE
Patinated and polished bronze

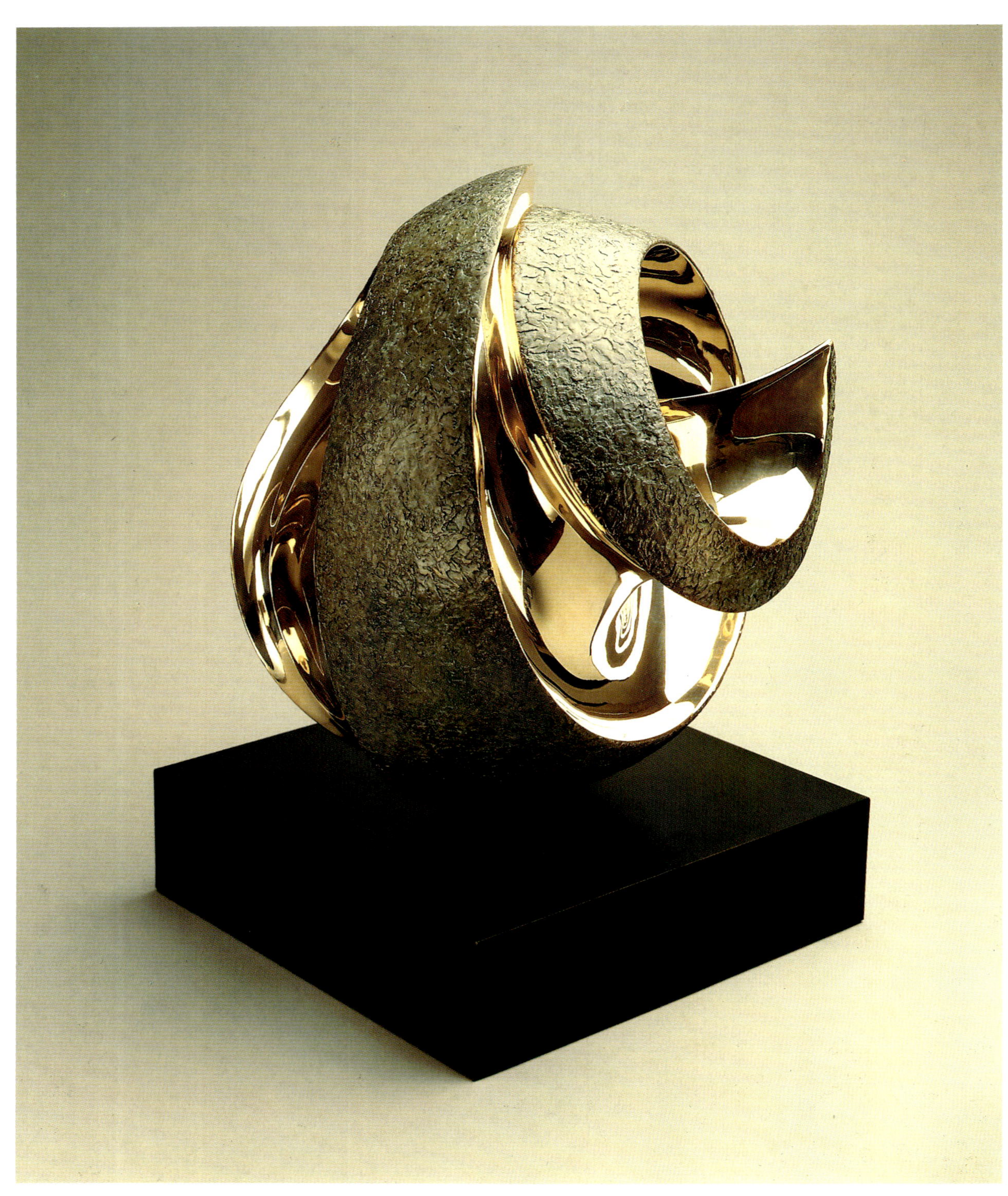

26. REFLETS DANS L'EAU
Patinated and polished bronze

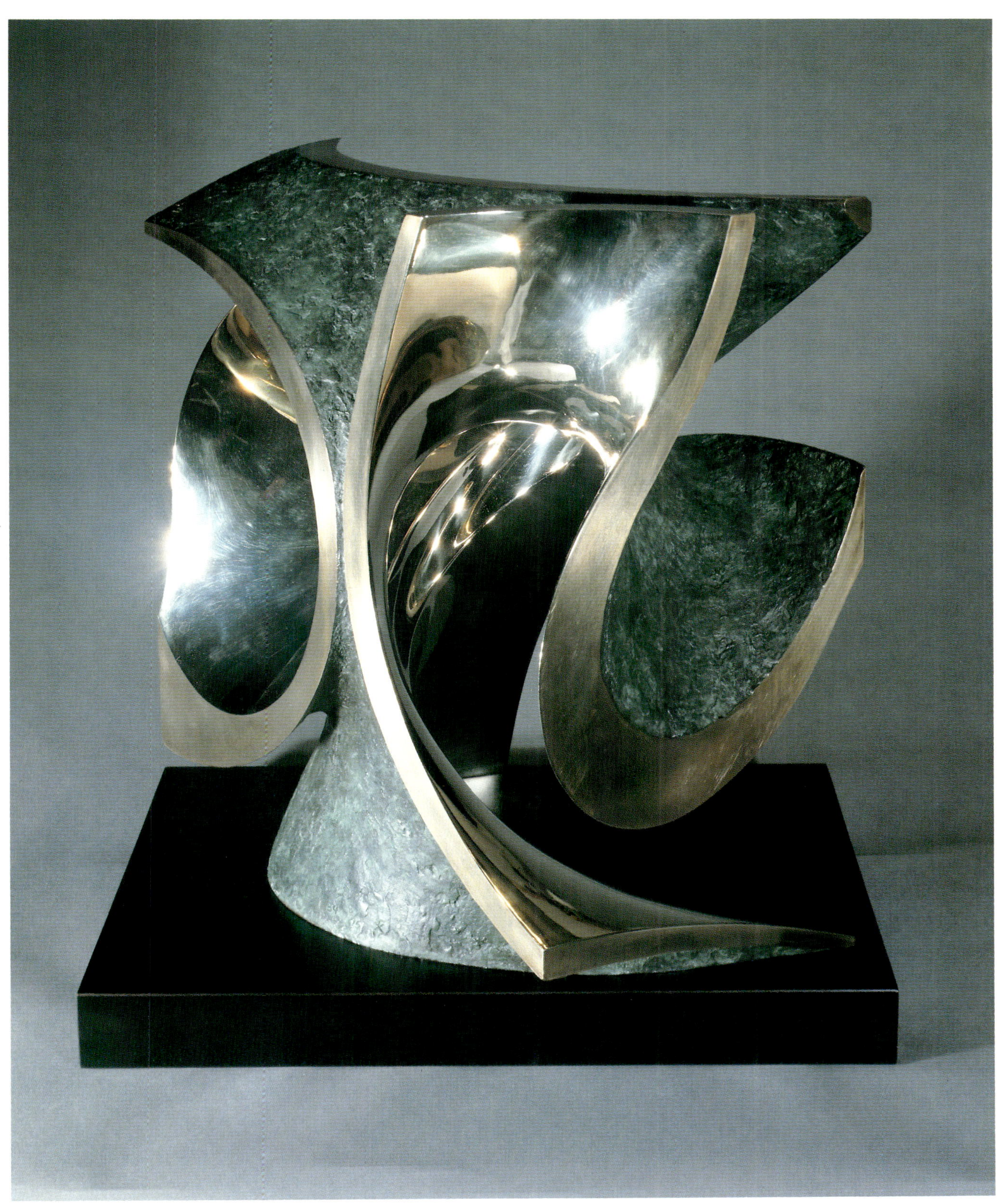

27. SARABANDE
Patinated and polished bronze

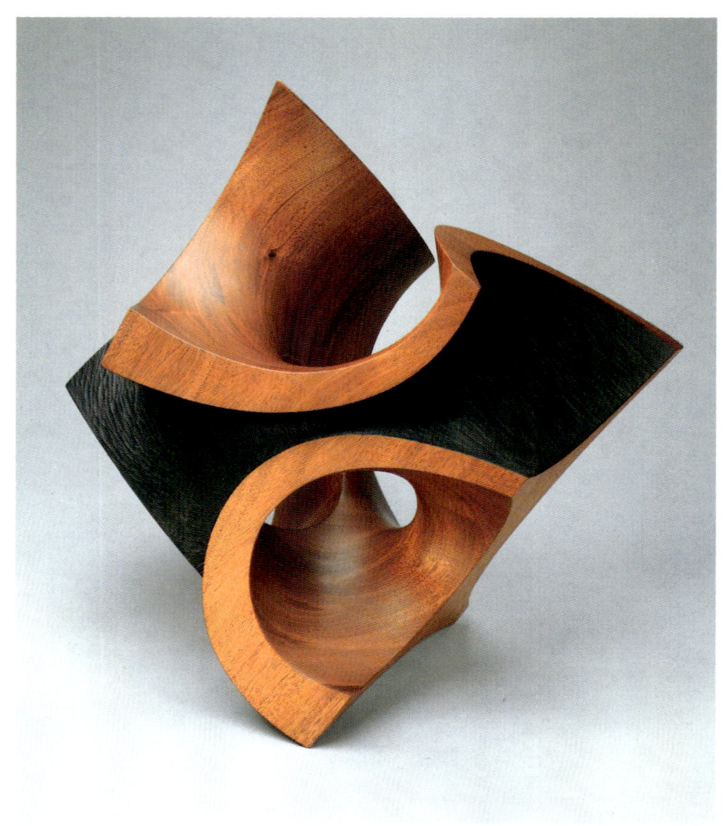

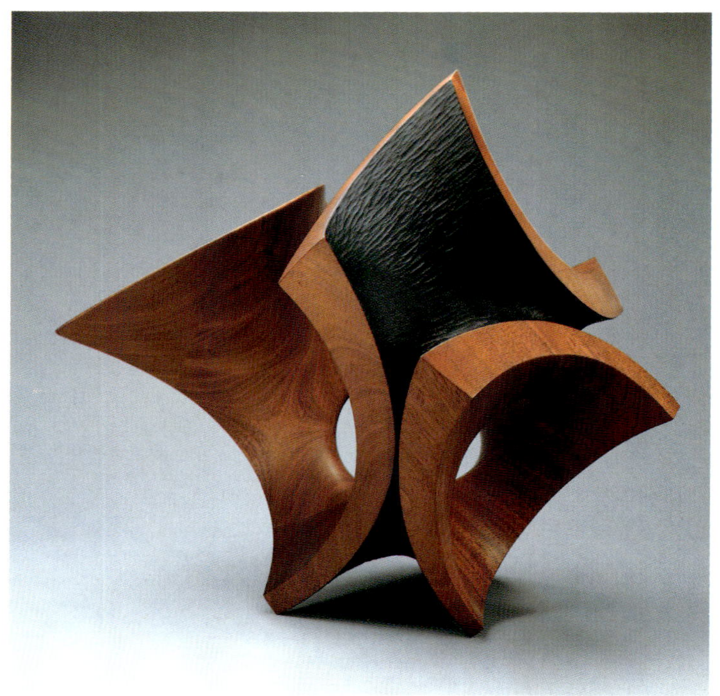

28. TEMPUS FUGIT
Mahogany polychrome

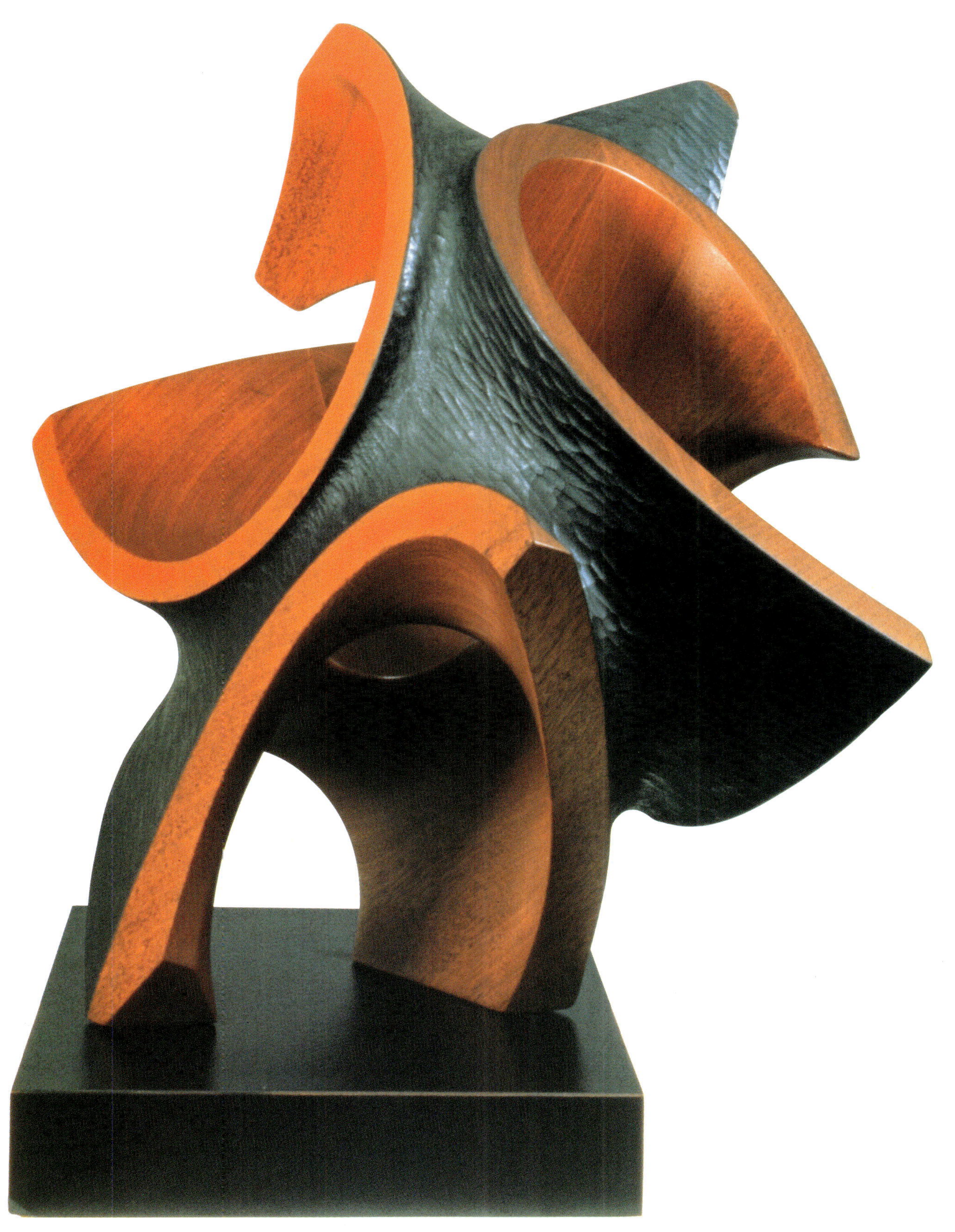

29. MIDNIGHT INDIGO
Mahogany polychrome

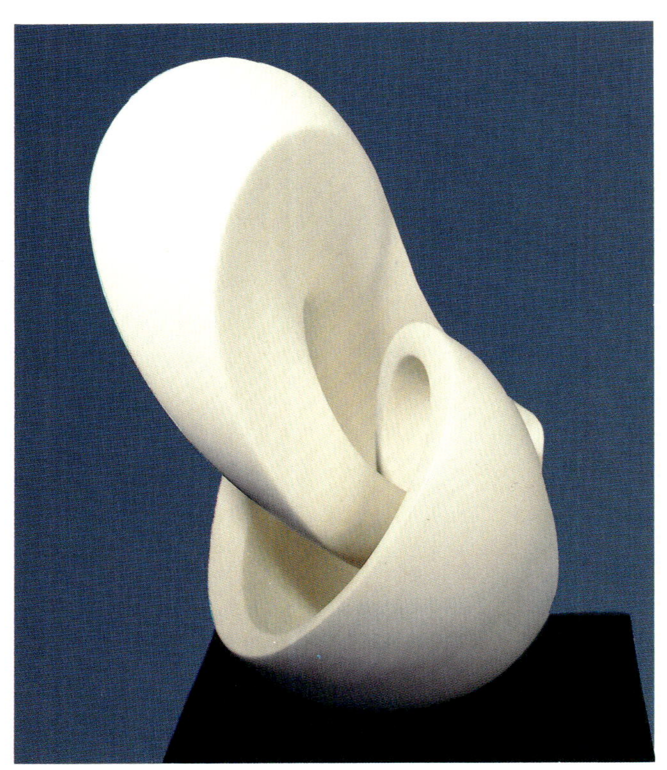

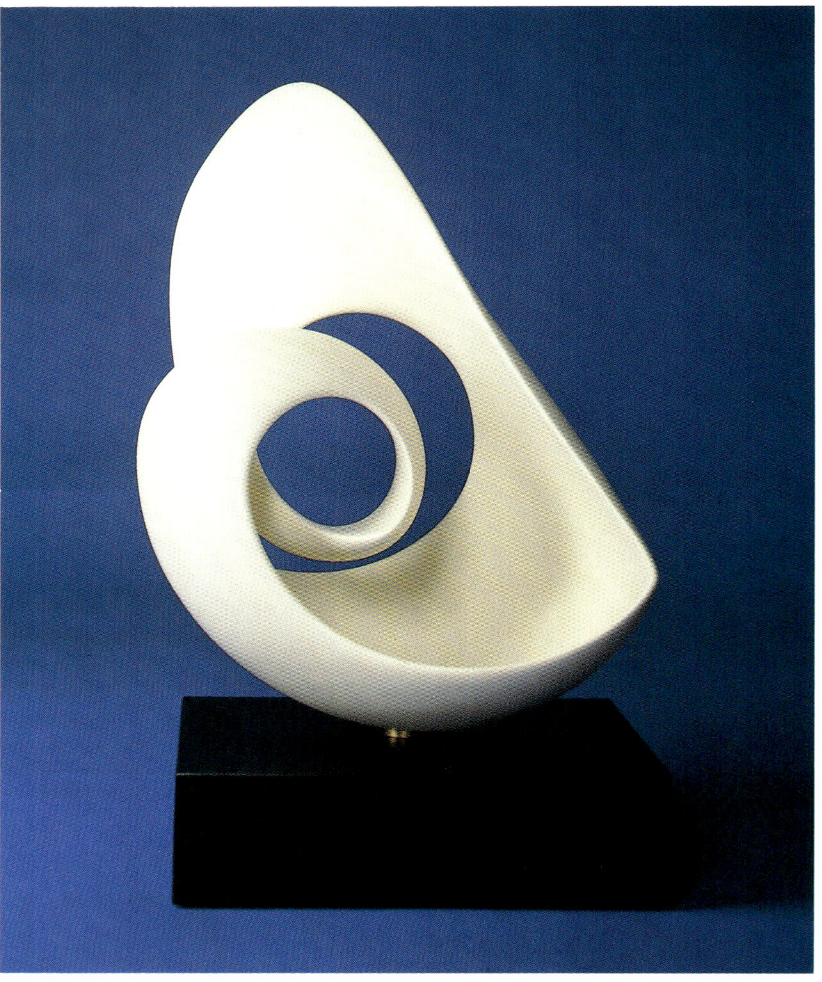

30. EMBOUCHURE
Ceramic

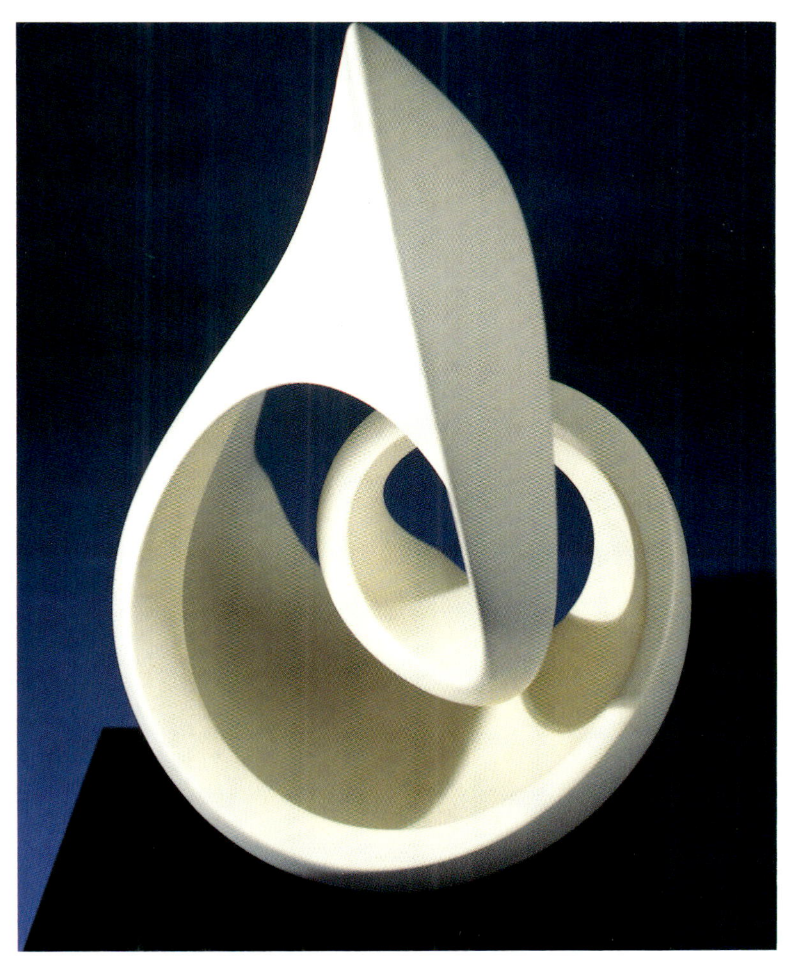

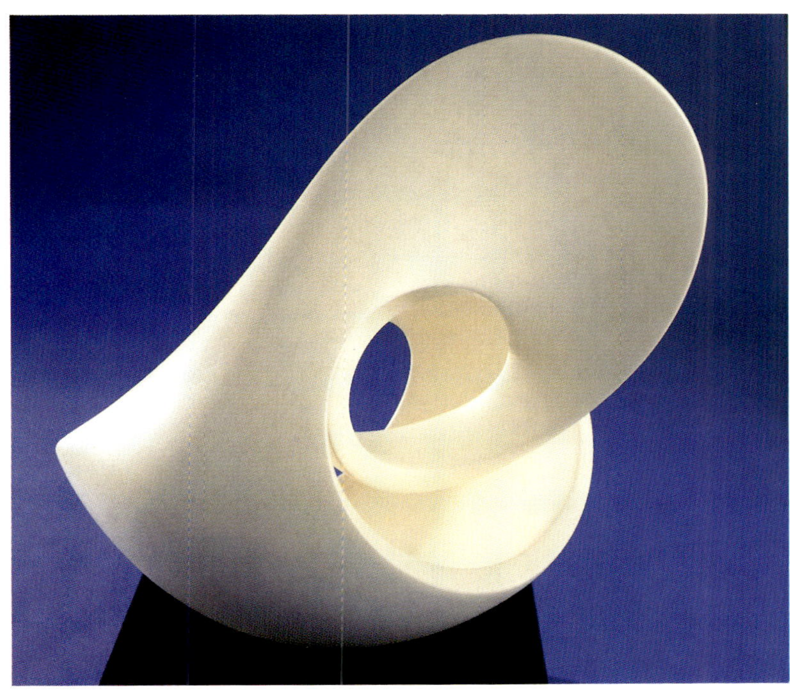

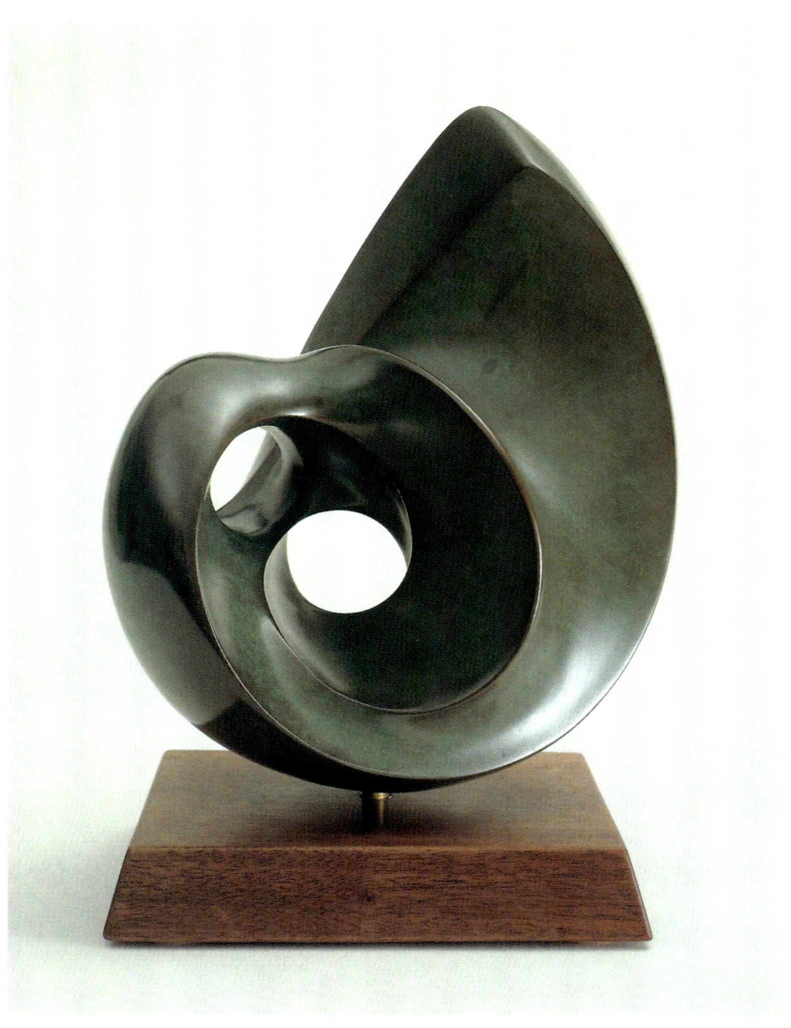

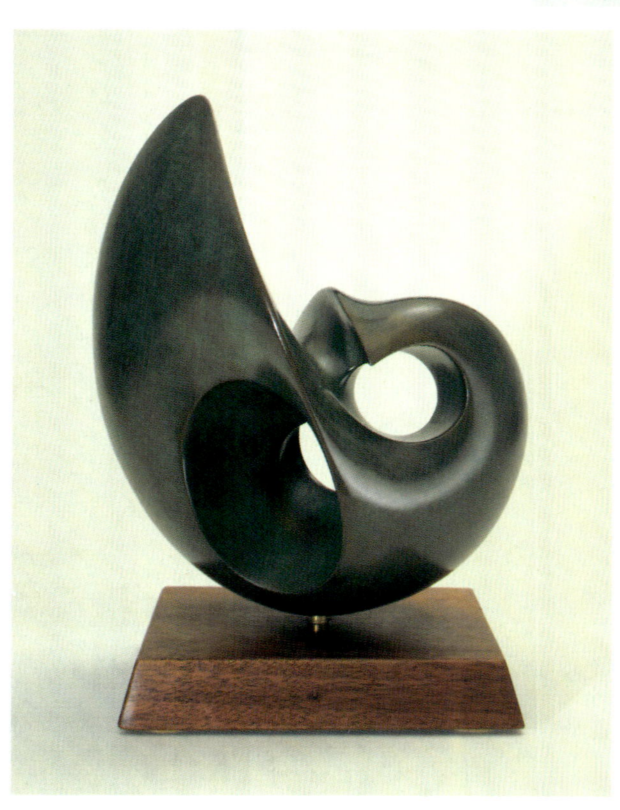

31. NOCTURNE
Patinated bronze

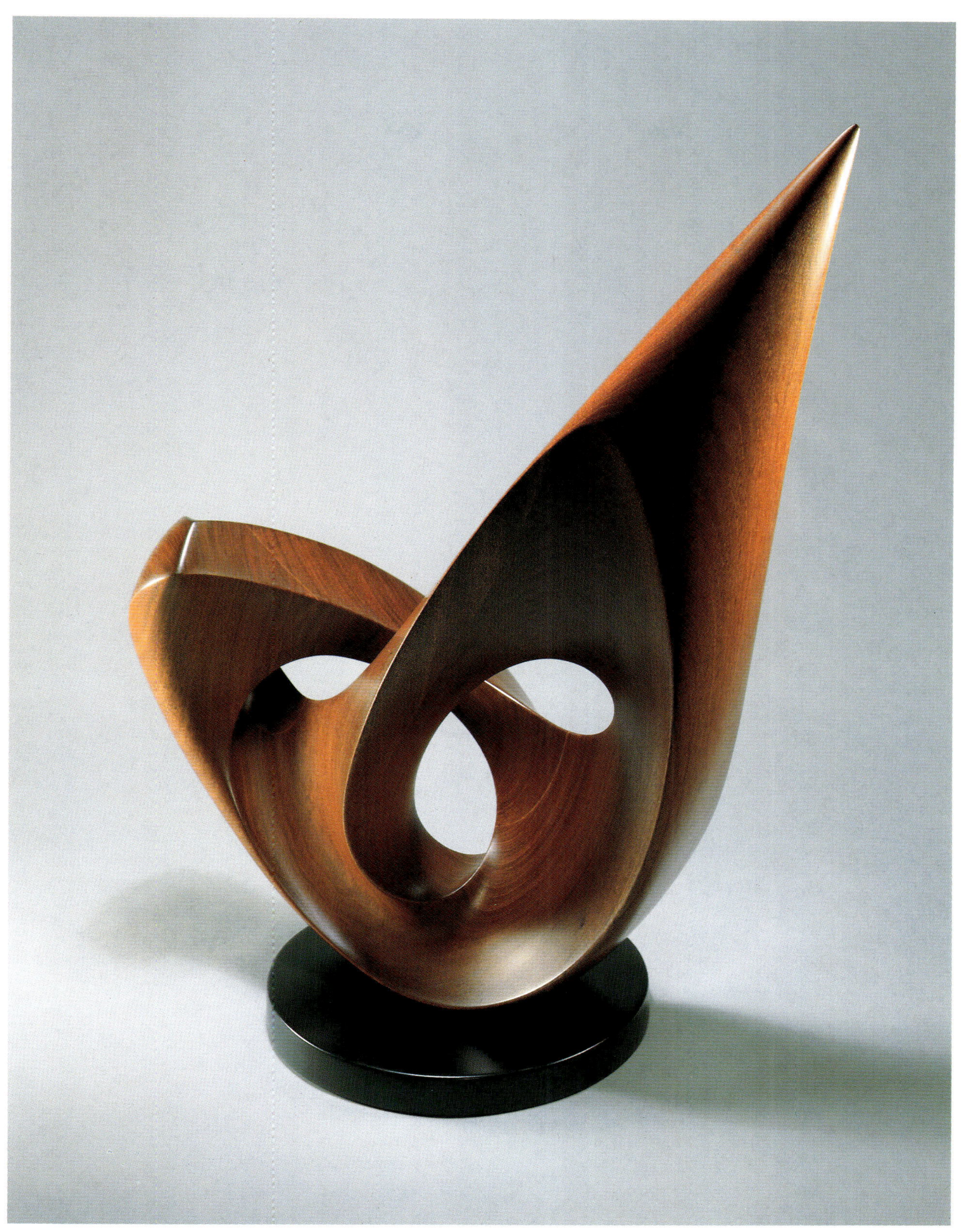

32. ENTRECHAT
Mahogany

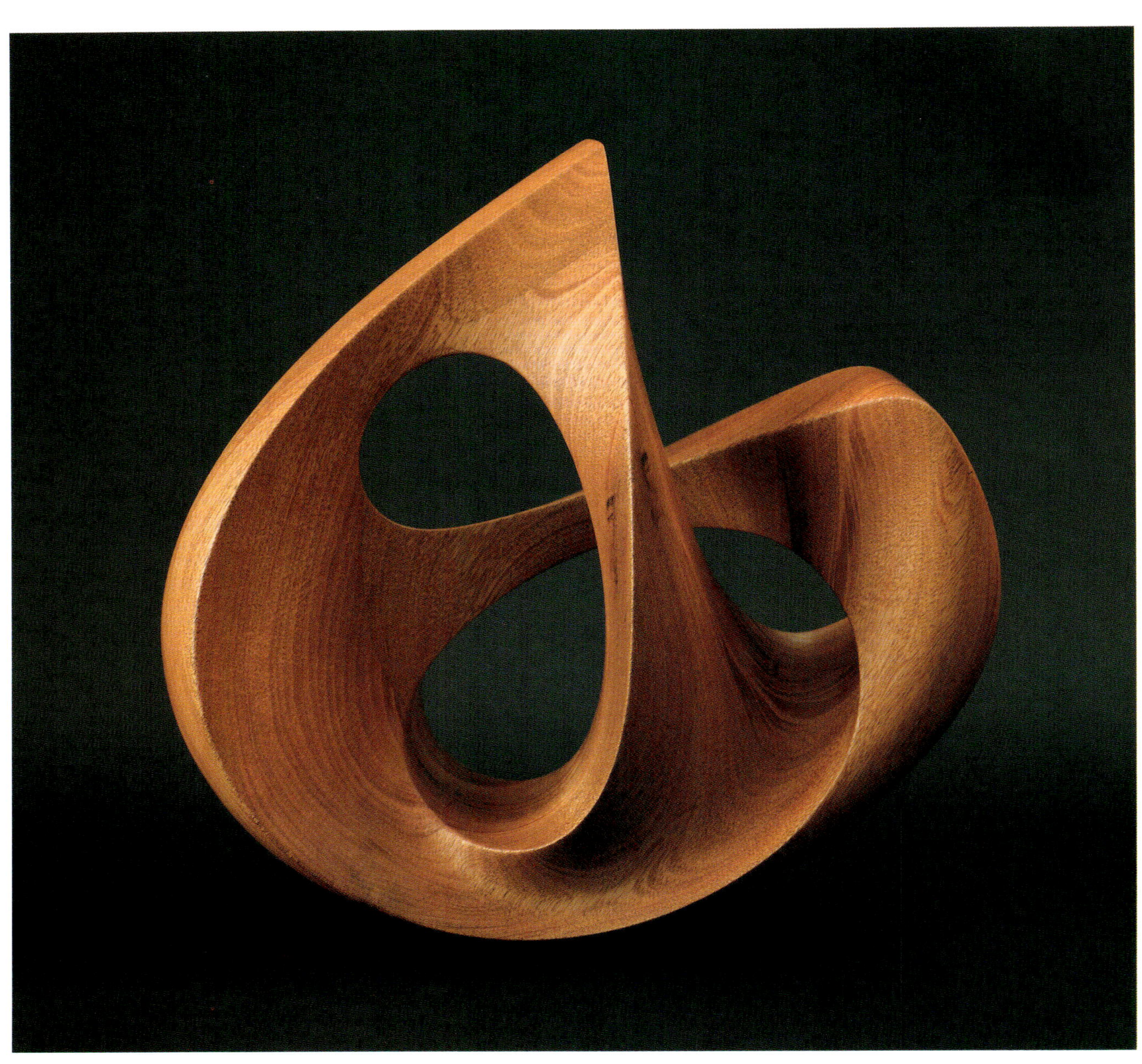

33. BOUREE
Mahogany

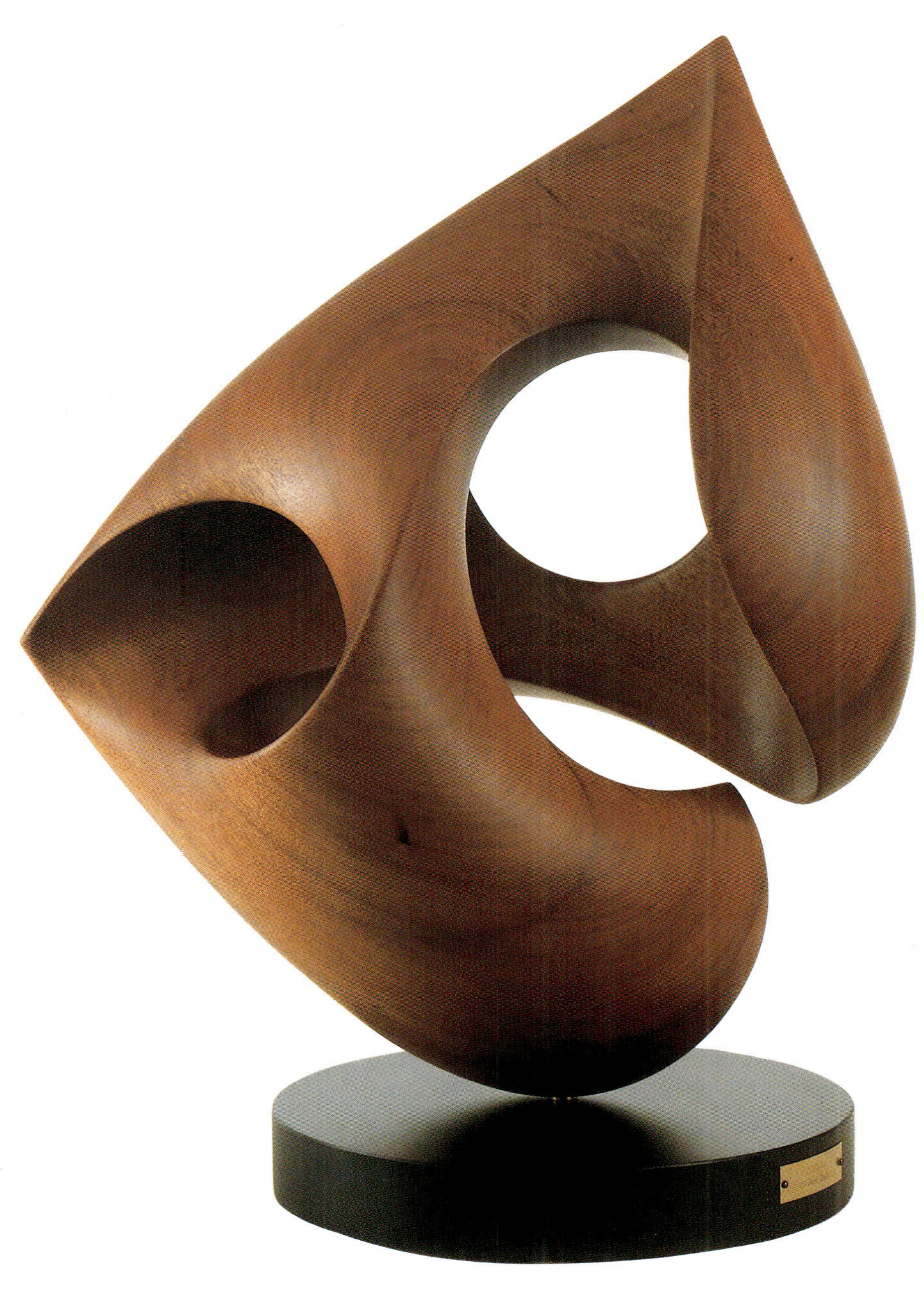

34. CAMERATA
Mahogany

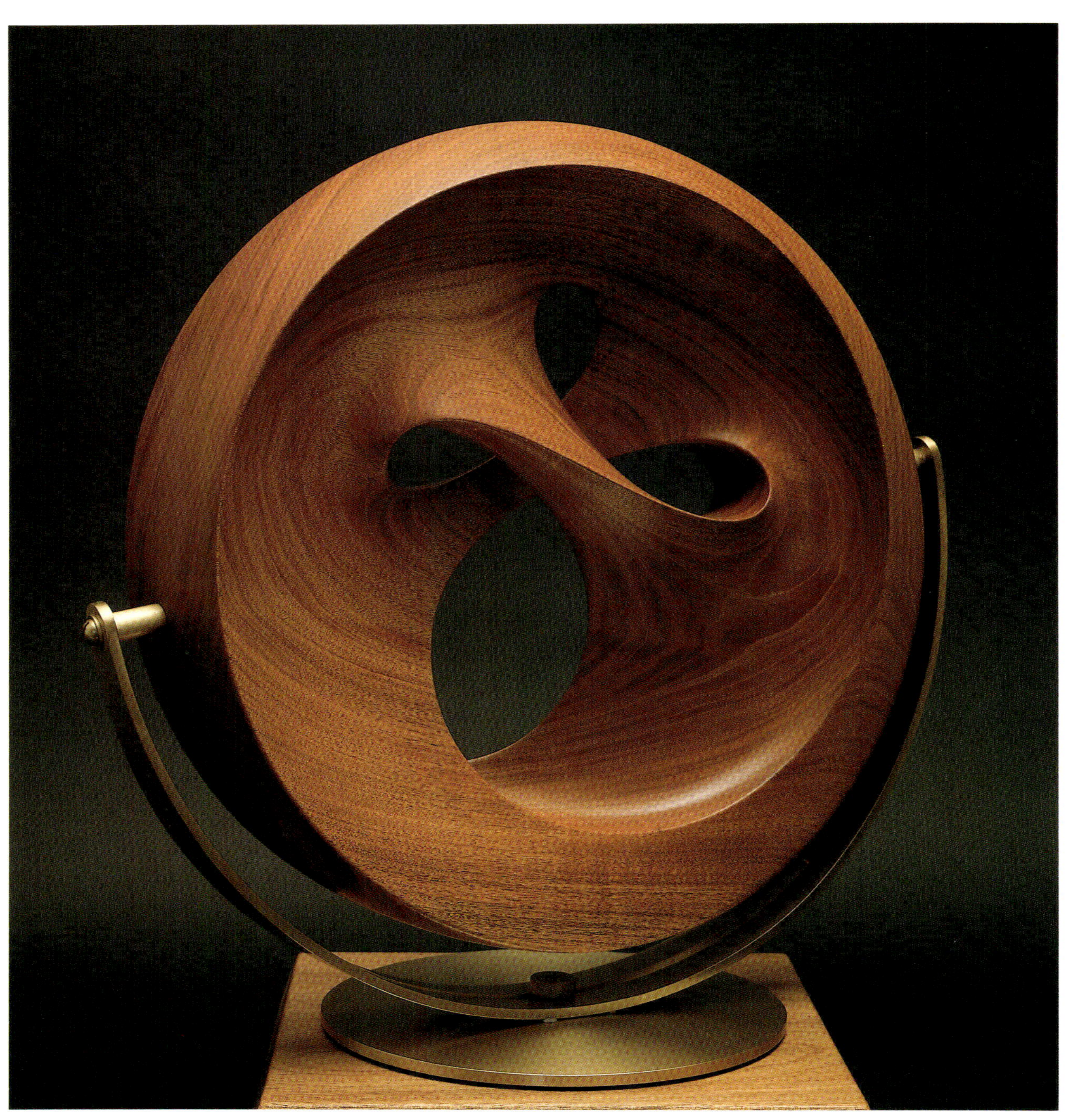

35. CLEFF VII
Mahogany and brass

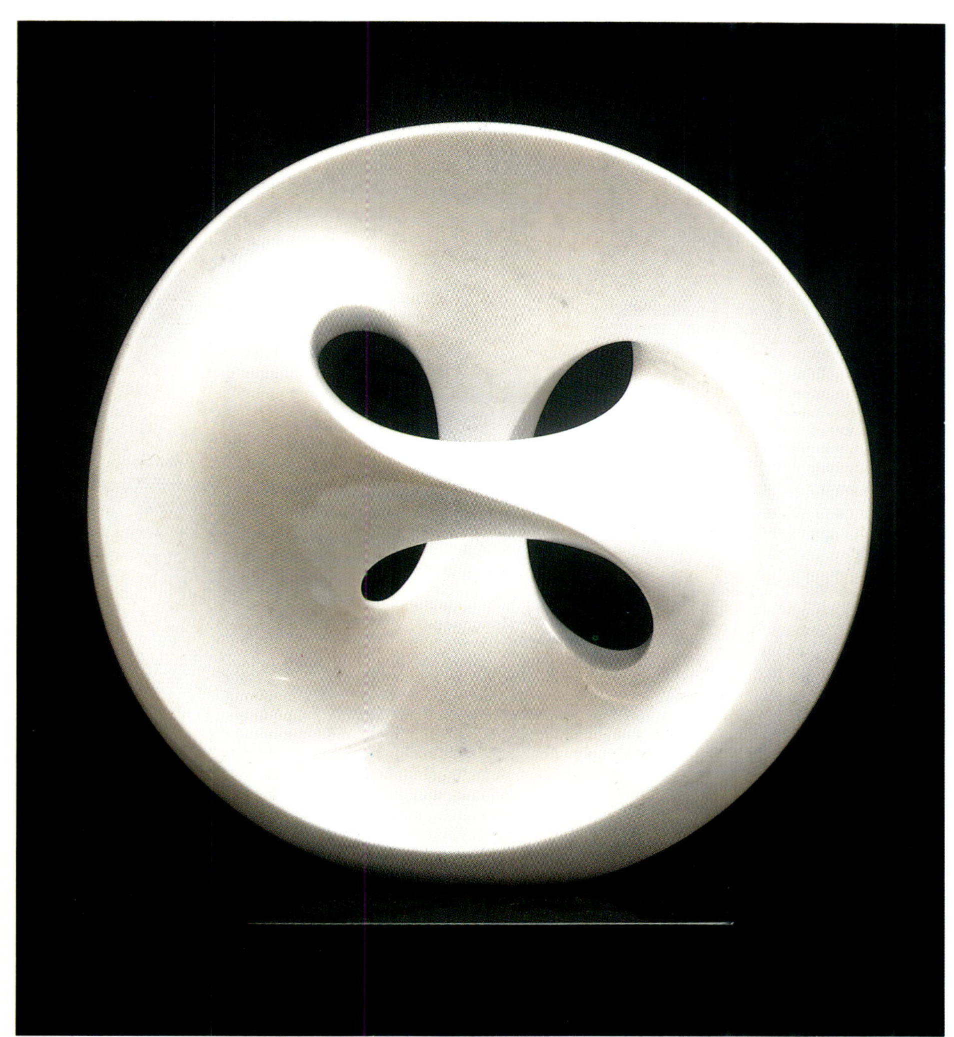

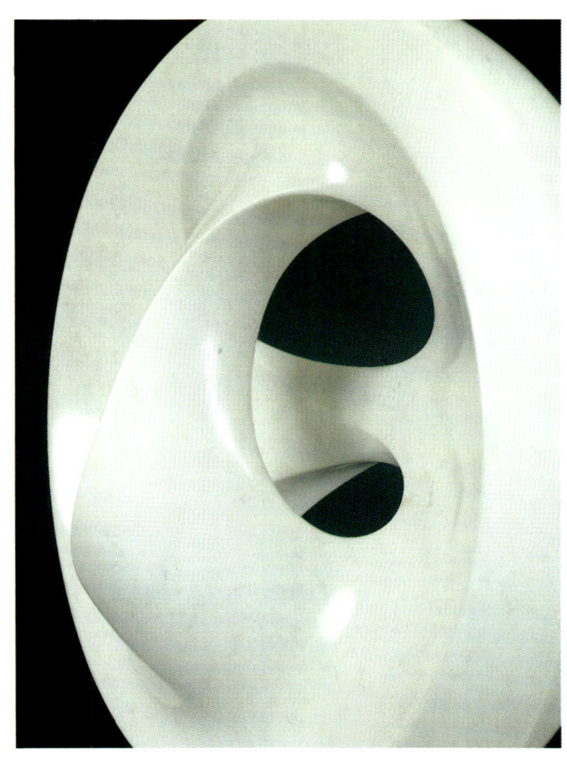

36. CADENZA
Marble

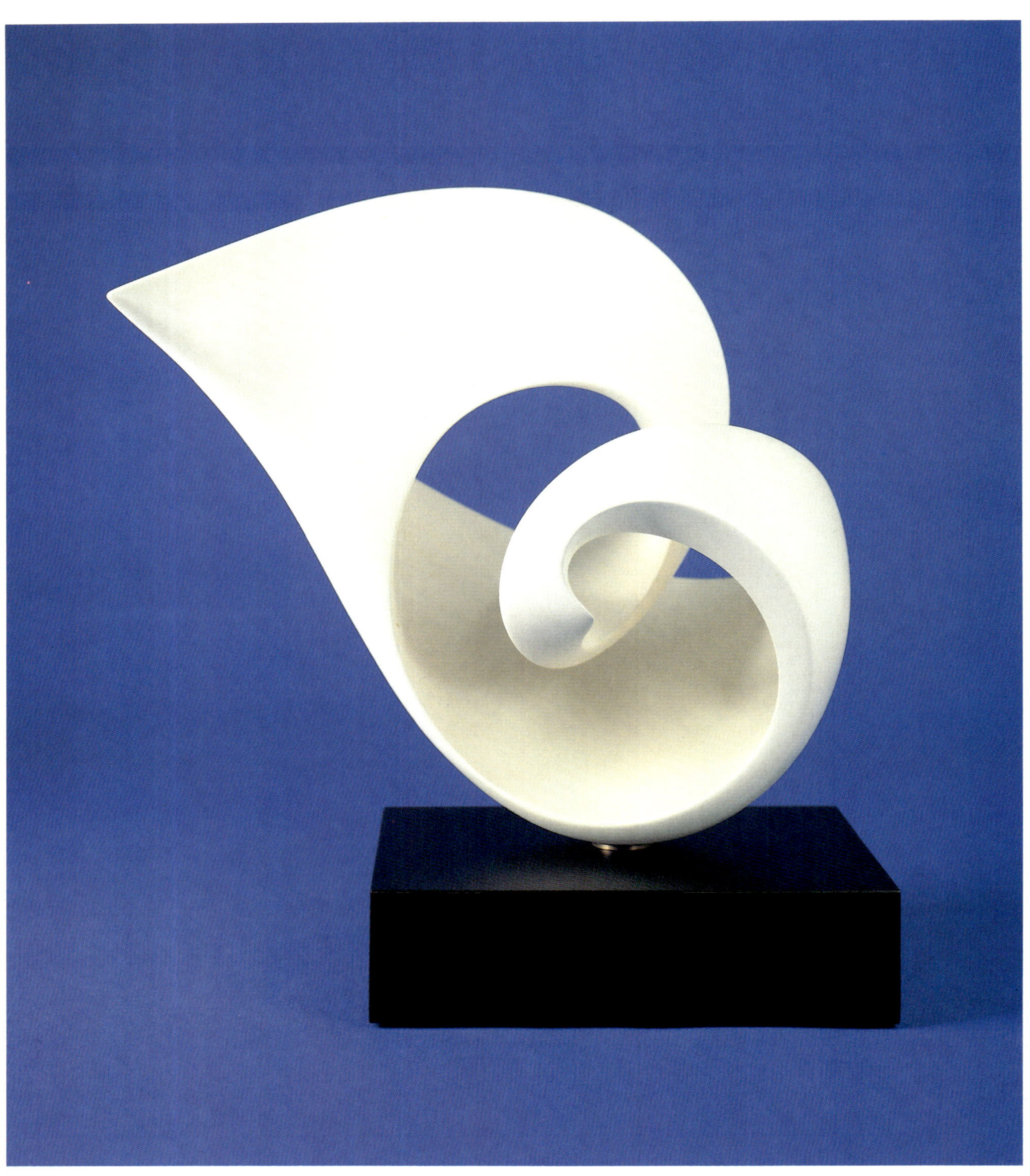

37. ESCHELLE
Ceramic

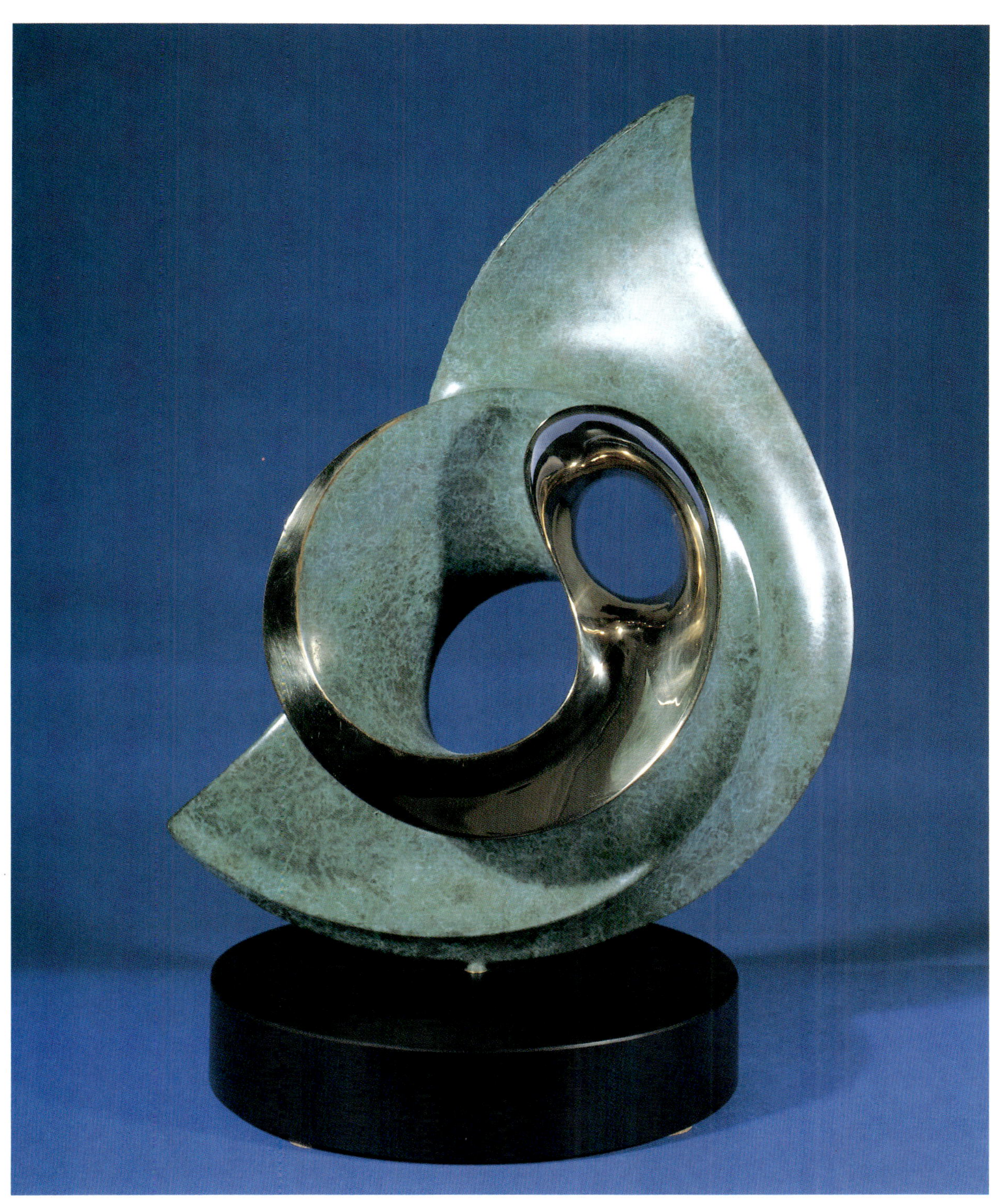

38. POISSON D'OR #15
Patinated and polished bronze

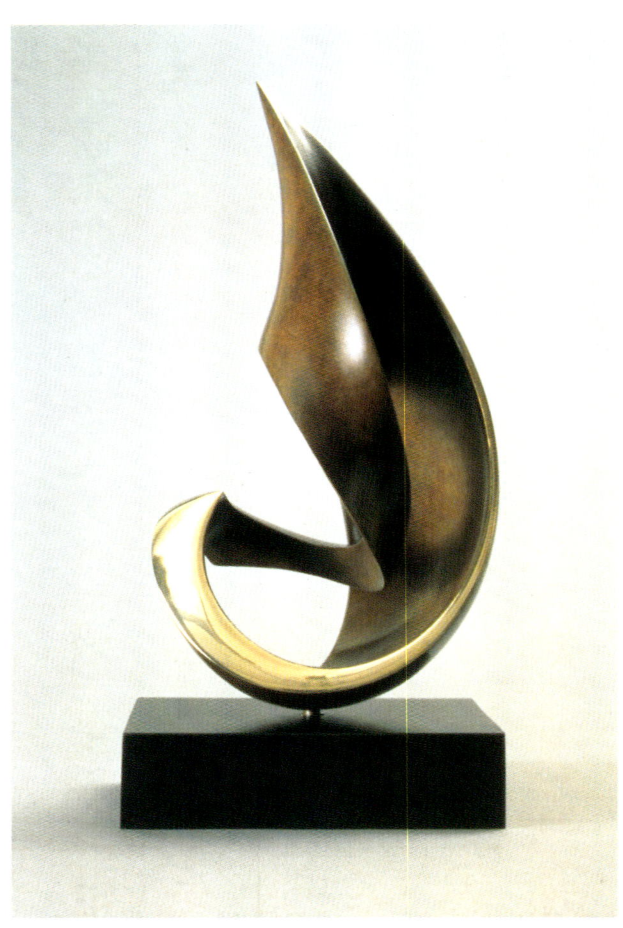

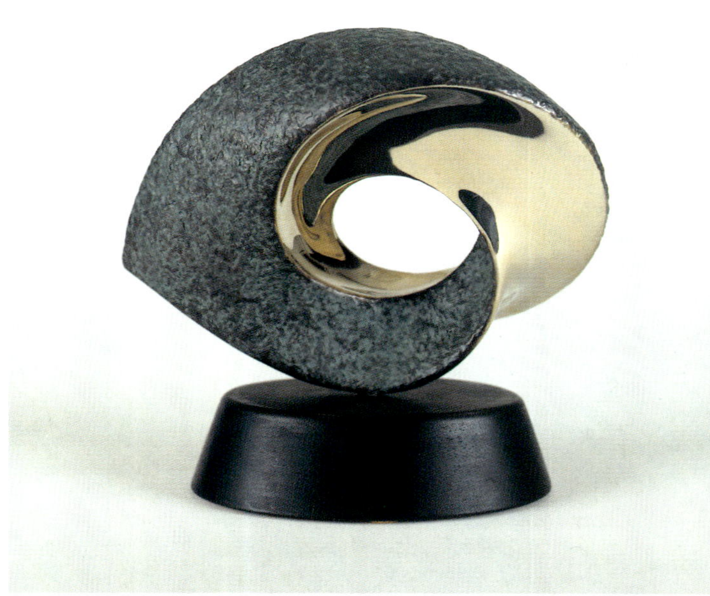

39. PSALMA I
Patinated and polished bronze

40. CONCERTO FOR STRINGS
Polished bronze

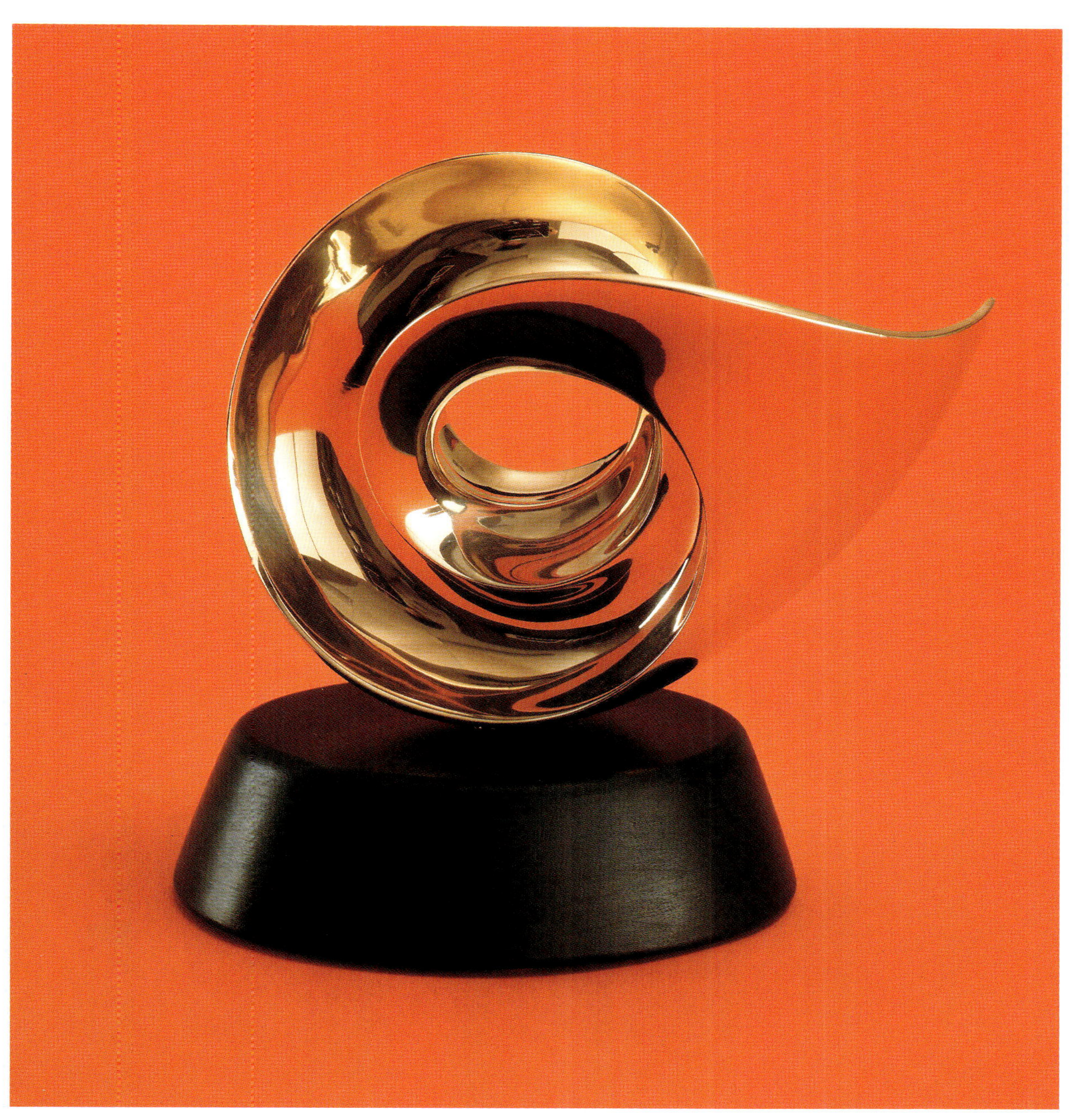

41. PSALMA II
Polished bronze

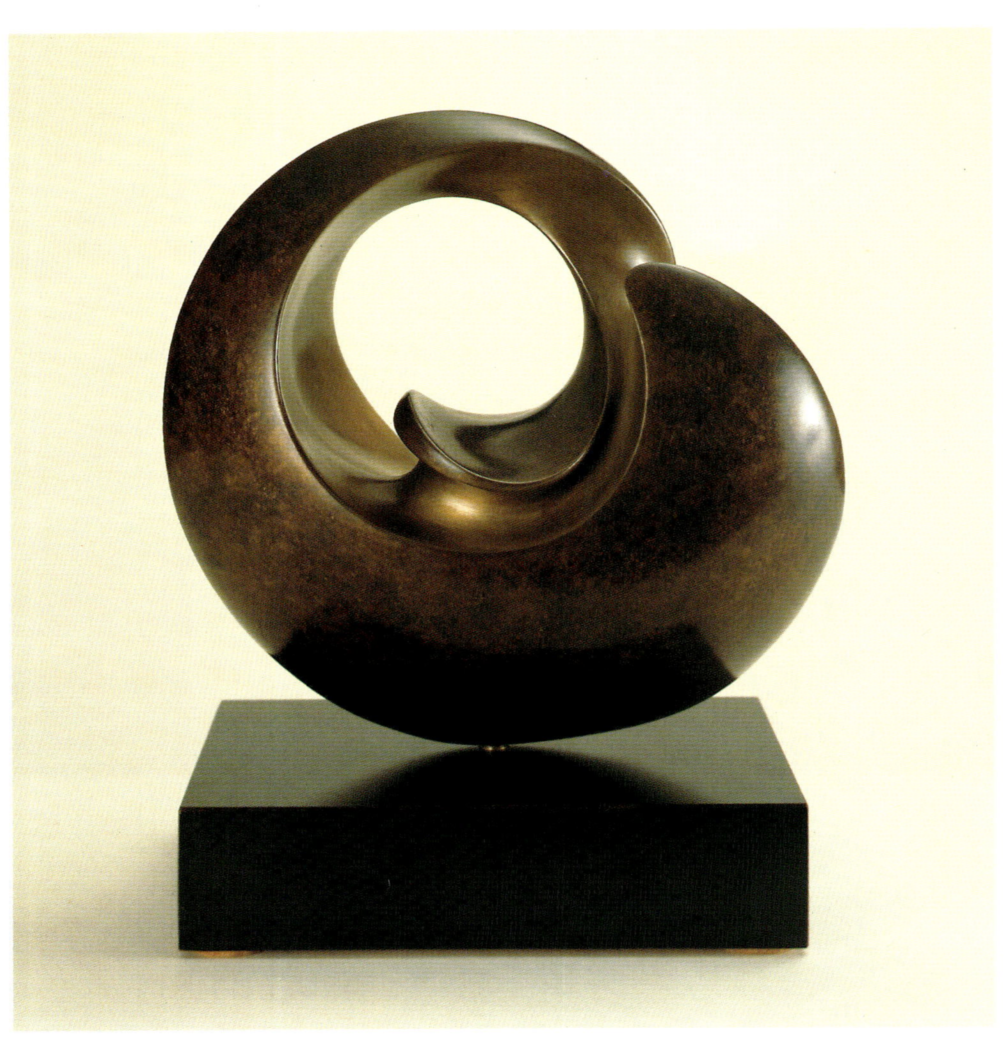

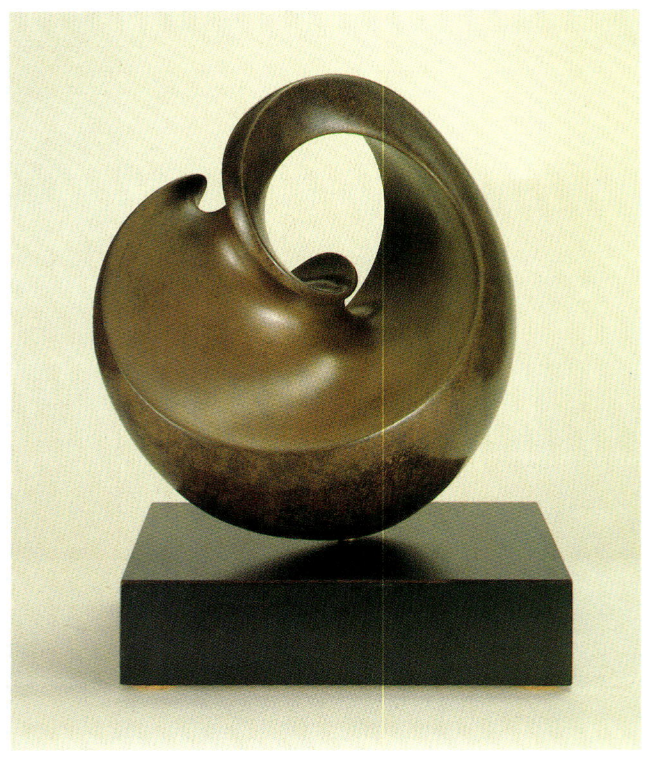

42. LULLABY
Patinated bronze

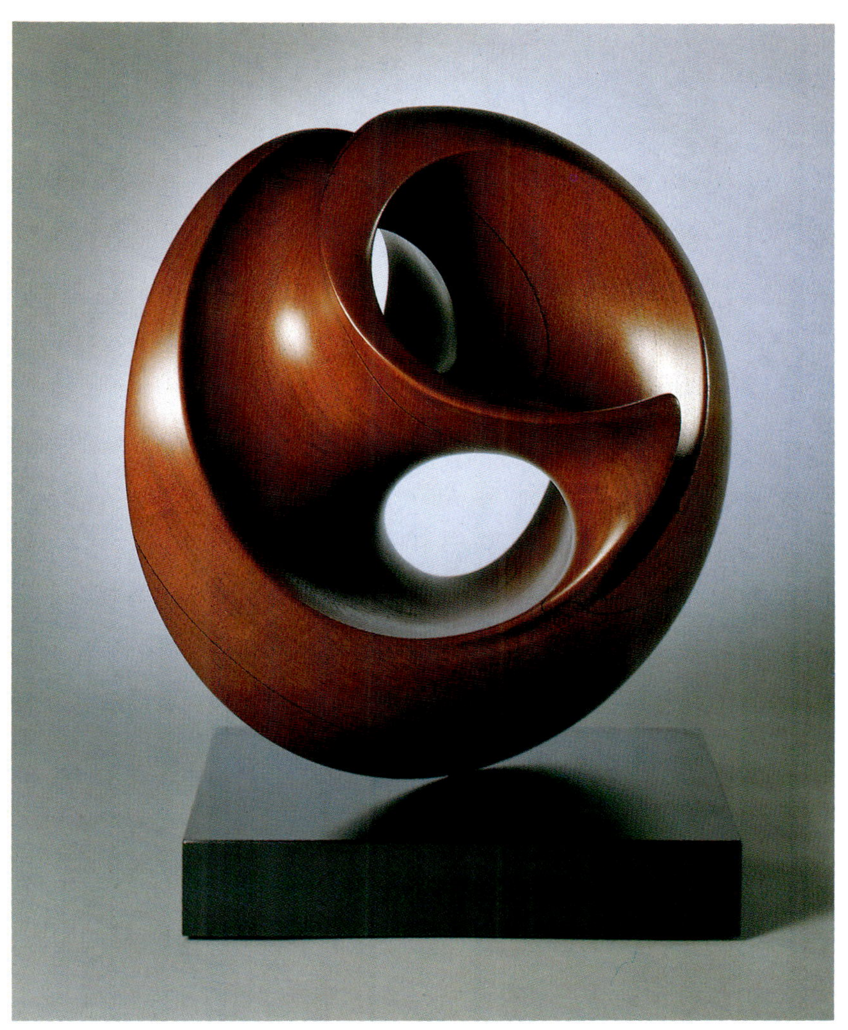

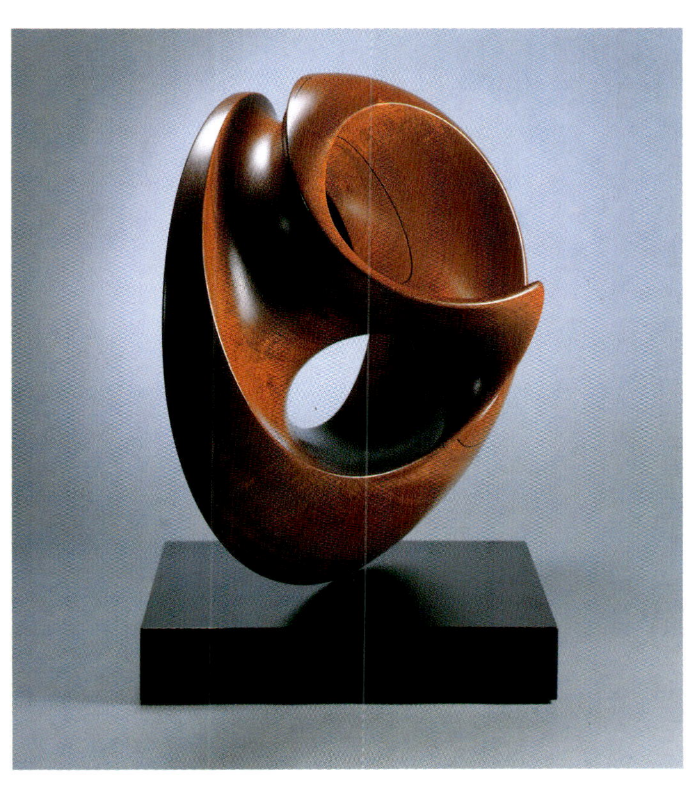

43. ENIGMATIC VARIATION #11
Mahogany

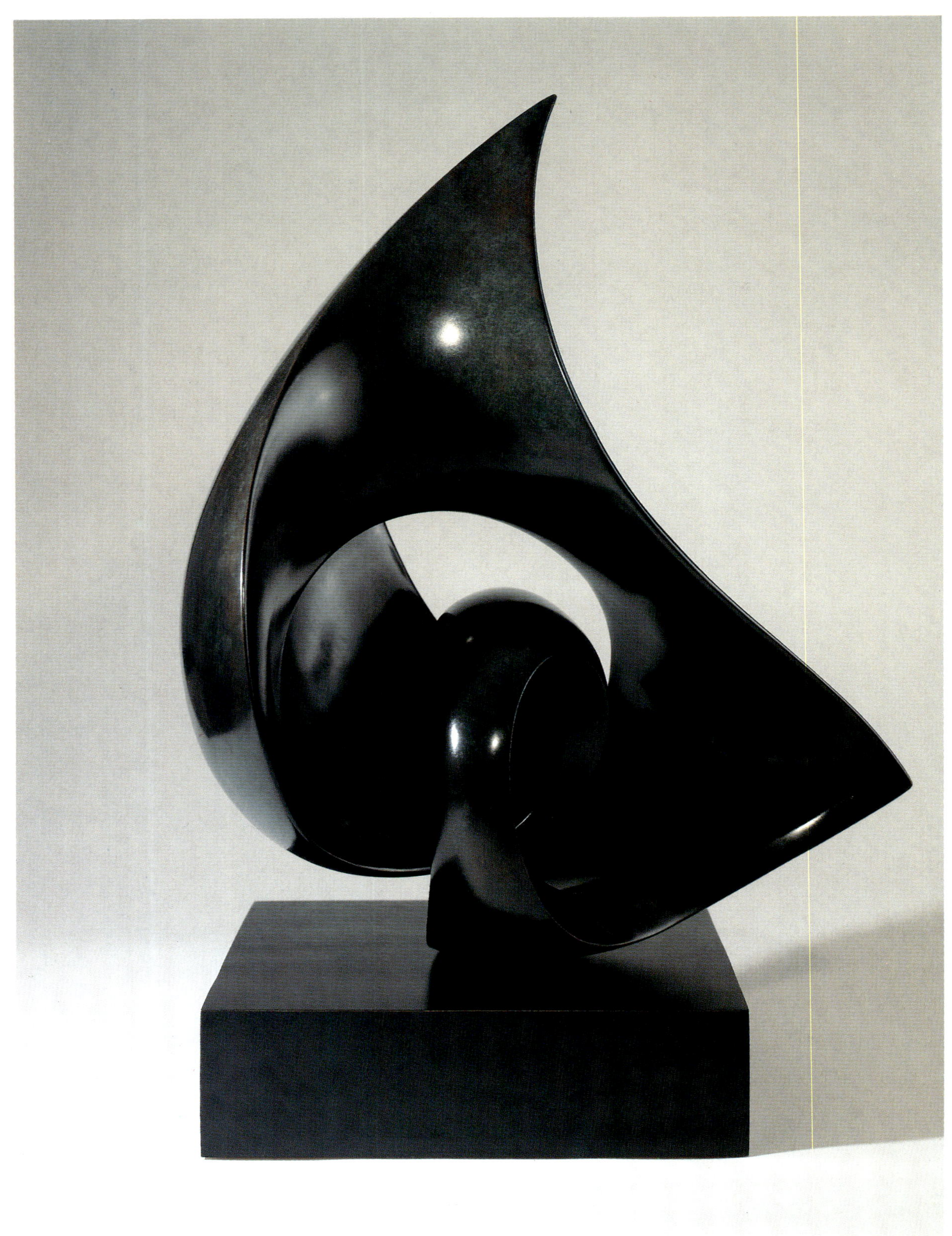

44. EROICA
Patinated bronze

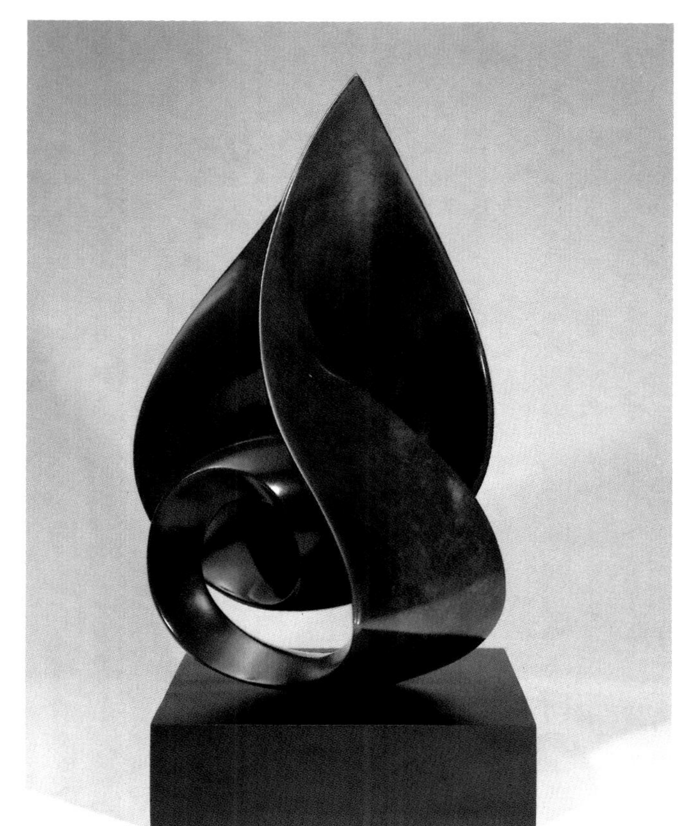

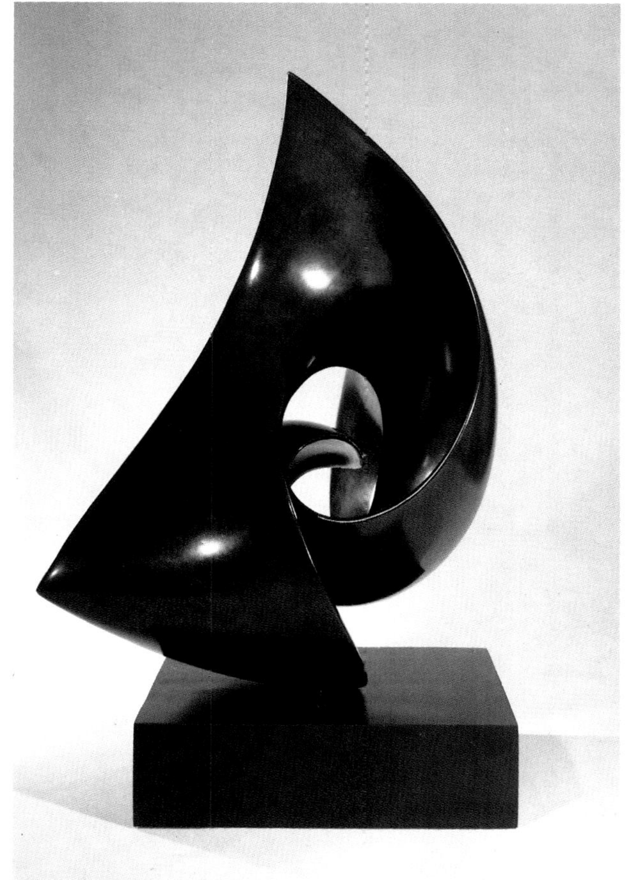

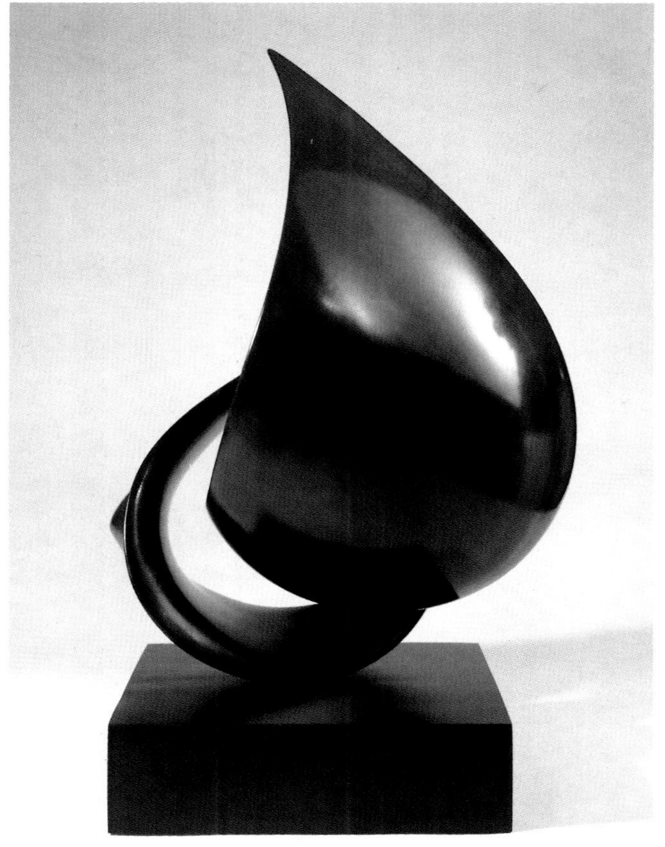

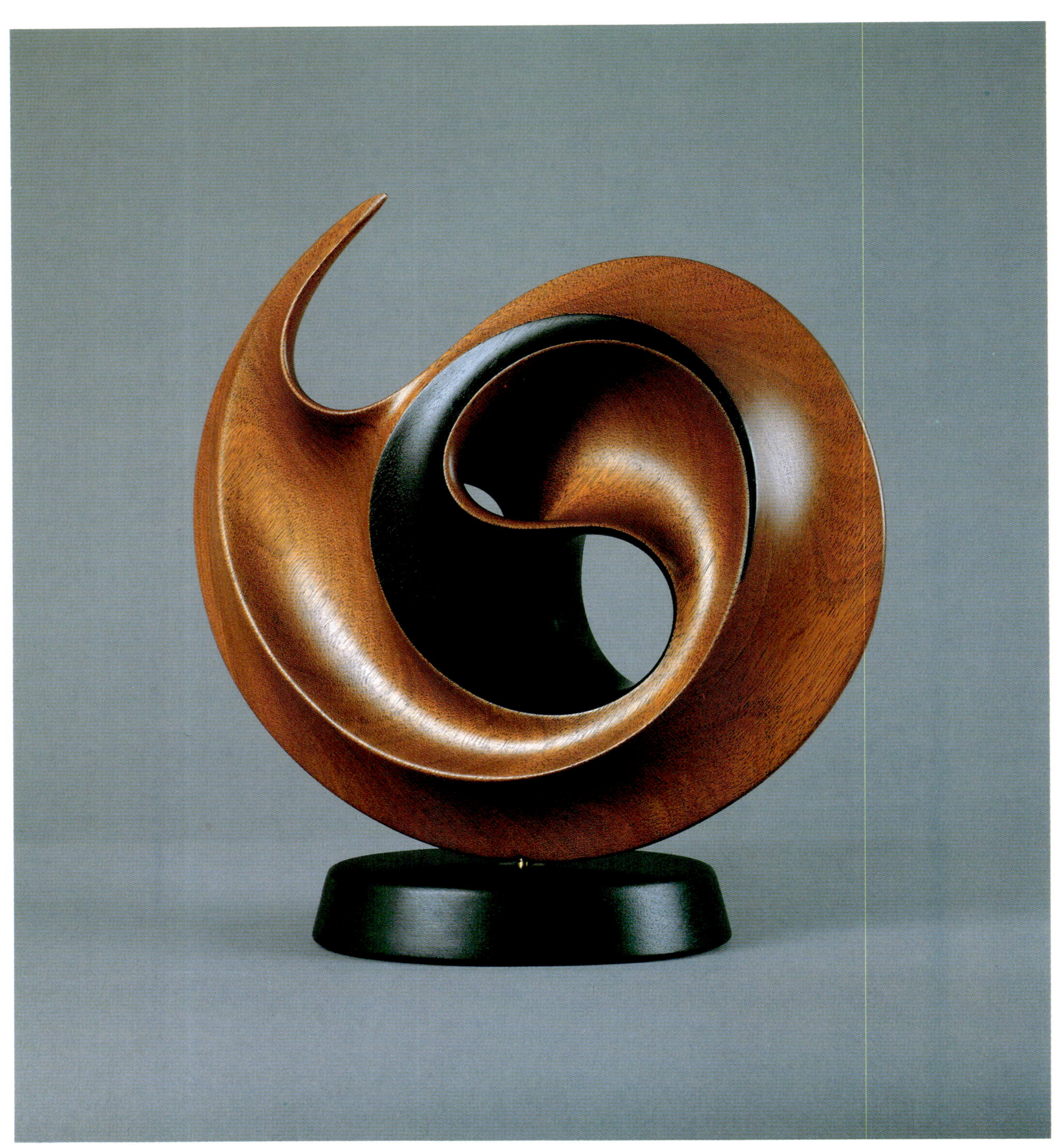

45. POISSON D'OR #14
Mahogany polychrome

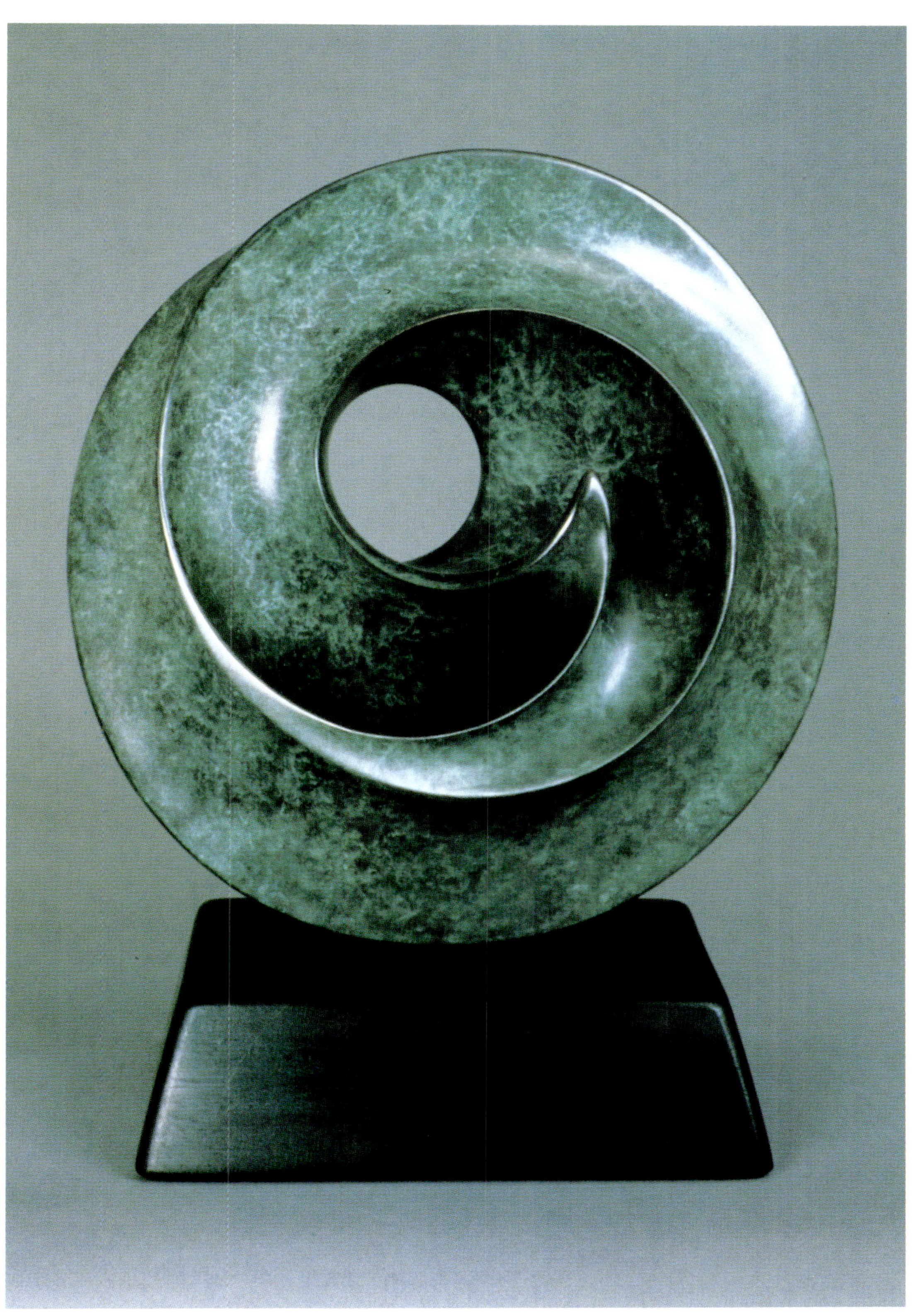

46. ENIGMATA
Patinated bronze

The Color Plates

COMMENTARY BY DAVID CHAMBERLAIN

Given measurements are for height only. Numbers in text refer to color plates.

front and back of jacket

Camerata
Patinated bronze
1987, edition 15 (A/P + 15 polished)
23″ or 58.2 cm

In literature and music *Camerata* means a small school of thought unto itself. This sculpture synthesizes many ideas I explored in other works into a new whole.

The elusive four-loop motif of the interior rapidly becomes the exterior framework of the design. The three corner points establish the sculpture's silhouette. At the lower point, there is an electric flux, a gravitational pull, between the rising solid form and the unfolding negative space above. This inner space has an inner fullness, suggestive of the womb.

I think of the piece as having powerful melody lines and broad overlapping harmonies. Within these broad movements are subtle hints and surprises.

frontispiece

Cadenza
Marble
1981
18″ or 45.54 cm

White marble has a cool, soft luster which is ethereal and unearthly — incredible for a rock which spent millions of years in the dark. As such, it has a mystical quality, capturing light and playing it back. The concave surfaces of white marble distill and intensify surrounding colors, and the convex surfaces reflect and expand them.

There is no room for error in carving marble - one tap too many and it is broken. *Cadenza* was wonderfully tricky to carve. It has four loops or two pairs of opposing ellipses. A rhythm, like the four-count in music, is created among them. The twist in its center had to be executed carefully. Once I had a distinct feel for the grain of the marble, it carved evenly.

Unlike bronze, marble cannot be stretched out into thin wispy forms, yet it is perfect for encouraging the eye to follow the flow of transitional surfaces and edges.

1. *Blumin'*
Patinated bronze
1985 edition 15 (6 patinated + 9 polished)
10½″ or 26.6 cm

If sculptures could talk among themselves, they would probably discuss their differences. Each piece reflects an idea or approach which, to the artist, was new enough to be worth exploring. Often several new concepts overlap in a single work. *Blumin'* represents a study of spiraling edges which grow and wrap around each other in several directions, developing from a single line extending outward and pulling back inward. The work was inspired by the life and death of an extraordinary young person.

2. *Sinfonietta*
Patinated bronze
1983, edition of 15 (9 patina a + 6 patina b)
18¾″ or 47.4 cm
Collections: McKissick Museum of Art, Columbia, South Carolina; Muskegan Museum of Art, Muskegan, Michigan; Colorado Springs Fine Arts Center and Museum, Colorado Springs, Colorado

Sinfonietta was inspired by a dream of three points in space appearing like a constellation. Three is a magical number; life is rich with trinities. It was exciting to sketch and shape this image from my subconscious. This work, *Embryons*, *Eroica*, and *Parfums de la Nūit* are metaphysical studies of points in space and time. As we alter our viewing perspective, these reference points change in relation to each other. The shifting views or illusions challenge our sense of reality, evoking the dream world from which it all began. We might ask what is more real - our visions of the work or the sculpture itself.

3. *A Une Passante*
Patinated bronze
1986, edition 15 (9 patina a + 6 patina b)
14″ or 35.4 cm
Collections: Gibson Gallery & Museum, SUNY Potsdam, N.Y.

A Une Passante literally means "as one passes by." I wanted the curving, wing-like forms of this sculpture to suggest the variety of passages we make in our lives.

A Une Passante's mottled verdant patina is made of greens, blues, and grays over a tawny bronze undertone. It changes with the light. The patina is applied under heat with a smokeless gas torch. Each color is created by oxidizing a chemical solution dabbed on with a soft brush. The acid solutions must be applied at specific strengths, speeds, and temperatures. The patinists, chemists, and I work closely together at the foundry to create these special formulas. They are registered in my name and are available only on these bronzes.

4. *A Cappella*
Polished bronze
1983, edition 15
10″ or 25.3 cm

All my life, I have been involved in *a cappella* music — the ensemble singing of intricate harmonies without instrumental or electronic enhancement. This pure form of vocalization involves both discipline and exultation, rendering a sound unlike any other.

This sculpture is inspired by four-part *a cappella* singing. The polished elements reflect each other as well as the ambience of the room, and blend together in various combinations of line and form in solos, duets, trios, and as a quartet. The harmonic surfaces transit from convex to ribbon-like to concave, and the meter of the lyrical edges varies accordingly. As the piece is rotated, the overall silhouette changes with the perspective of the viewer.

5. *Concerto for Woodwind*
Patinated bronze
1988, edition 15
11½″ or 22.77 cm.

6. *Mazurka*
Polished bronze
1983, A/P
9″ or 22.77 cm
Collections: Johnson
Museum of Art, Ithaca, New York

7. *Mazurka*
Patinated bronze
1983, edition 15
9″ or 22.77 cm
Collections: Jewett Museum of Art, Wellesley, Massachusetts

8. *Concerto for Brass*
Polished bronze
1988, edition 15
11½″ or 29.1 cm

9. *Festivale*
Polished bronze
1982, edition 15 (A/P, polished + 15 patinated)
12″ or 30 36 cm
Collections: Cheekwood Botanical Gardens and Fine Arts Center, Nashville, Tennessee.

I began working with spirals as a means to transcend predictable shapes. The spirals I felt most drawn to were always the ones which changed geometry mid-stream, those which broke away from standard mathematical formulas. I discovered that three-dimensional spirals are even more provocative because they change formulas as the viewing perspective changes. In this era of computer-aided design, it is exciting to work with organic spirals which defy being mathematically coded and reproduced.

Festivale investigates what three-dimensional spirals can do when woven together. The main spiral goes simply from top point to upper side point. This is combined with a pattern of two spirals put together which originates at the lower side point. This heart-shaped pattern is actually an illusion; it is really a spiraling edge passing through and around itself twice, bending in the middle at this third point of reference.

10. *Heartsong*
Polished bronze
1984, edition 15 (12 polished, 3 patinated, A/P)
14″ or 35.42 cm

11. *Parfums De La Nuit*
Patinated bronze
1985, edition 15 (9 patina a + 6 patina b)
14⅜″ or 36.37 cm

12. *Scheherezade*
Mahogany
1981
17″ or 43 cm

Mahogany is a rare, precious resource in today's environment. I treat this wood with reverence and respect. Its unique luster captures and refracts light. By working with concave surfaces at angles which mirror the source light, it is possible to create areas which glow. In *Scheherezade* the glow often originates in the innermost surfaces. Light is captured, concentrated, and then returned. It is almost as if the sculpture is alive.

My sculpture was inspired by Rimsky Korsakov's symphonic suite 'Scheherezade' which celebrates tales from *The Arabian Nights*.

13. *Enigmatic Variation #9*
Mahogany
1986
14½″ or 36.69 cm

I majored in architecture in college. The interiors of buildings interested me more than exteriors, perhaps because we inhabit these spaces. In making sculpture I wanted to retain this spatial intimacy by concentrating on hollows and openings. I still think of myself as an inhabitant of each sculpture I make, shrinking myself to move around and through the space.

In the *Enigmatic Variation* series, I explored the concept of two tunnel-like openings sharing the same walls as they wrap around themselves. The enigma is that we cannot perceive this flow readily.

14. *Akimbo*
Mahogany
1980
17″ or 43 cm

Wood is warm to the touch. It was alive once and has individual grain characteristics. It tells a story while you work it. Sometimes it even has a sense of humor. I select my own blocks and make them for each sculpture. All the carving is done here in the studio. The more I ponder and play with the design, the more I learn. The pieces take a long time to make so they become like old friends.

15. *Adagio*
Mahogany
1980
17″ or 43 cm

16. *Open Cleff*
Patinated bronze
1981, edition 15
11″ or 27.83 cm

17. *Quartetta*
Patinated bronze
1981, edition 15
13″ or 32.90 cm
Collections: Art Complex Museum, Duxbury, Massachusetts

18. *Poisson D'Or #15*
Mahogany polychrome
1987
15″ or 37.95 cm

19. *Rhapsody*
Patinated bronze
1982, edition 15
15″ or 37.95 cm
Collections: Nelson Museum of Art, Kansas City, Missouri; Delaware Museum of Art, Wilmington, Delaware; Smith College, Museum, Northampton, Massachusetts

20. *Embryons*
Patinated bronze
1986, edition 15 (9 patina a + 6 patina b)
14″ or 35.42 cm

21. *Moku No Kaze*
Mahogany
1984
14″ or 35.42 cm

22. *Poisson D'Or #10*
Patinated and polished bronze
1987, edition 15 (9 patina a + 6 patina b)
25″ or 63.25 cm

23. *Poisson D'Or #10*
Mahogany
1987
25″ or 63.25 cm

The playful, shadowy, mysterious rhythms of Debussy's piano compositions partly inspired the *Poisson D'Or* series.

I think of each of my works as having many "faces." As you turn it, its personality changes. In *Poisson D'Or # 10*, one face is sensuous and fluid. Its inner curves are shiny, buffed highly with jeweler's rouges. Light is drawn into the core, mirroring the surroundings and contrasting the outer curves of dark green patina. The opposing face has two holes or eyes. It has a tribal starkness that surprises the viewer.

24. *Balletta*
Patinated and polished bronze
1985, edition 15 (9 patina a + 6 patina b)
11″ or 27.83 cm

25. *Ballade*
Patinated bronze
1984, edition 15 (9 patina a + 6 patina b)
10″ or 25.30 cm

Sometimes the purest forms are the most challenging to create. The tuning up can take forever. The elemental crux of *Ballade* is a single edge spiraling from one point in space to another. This edge generates polished transitional surfaces which are held in place within a spherical format. Like a Haiku, *Ballade* is a form reduced to essence and infinite complexity.

26. *Reflets Dans L'Eau*
Patinated and polished bronze
1986, edition 15 (9 patina a + 6 patina b)
17″ or 43 cm

27. *Sarabande*
Patinated and polished bronze
1983, edition 15 (9 patina a + 6 patina b)
16″ or 40.48 cm

28. *Tempus Fugit*
Mahogany polychrome
1984
17″ or 43.00 cm
Collections: Currier Gallery and Museum, Manchester, New Hampshire

29. *Midnight Indigo*
Mahogany polychrome
1984
20½″ or 51.87 cm

Jazz is rich with syncopation. I explored this concept visually in a group of sculptures titled *The Jazz Series*, inspired by composers like Duke Ellington and Dave Brubeck. Syncopation in a four-beat musical phrase shifts the accent from the expected downbeat to a weak or off beat. I create this same sense of surprise through asymmetrical composition.

In *Midnight Indigo*, the melodic line appears as the interior edge flowing through and around the piece. The natural grain of the wood carries the inner melody, wrapped by the black, bark-like outer surfaces which provide the contrasting harmonies. By cutting off most of the enclosing exterior forms, the sculpture takes on an open, jaunty character, revealing a visible group of related interior forms.

30. *Embouchure*
    Ceramic
    1984
    17″ or 43 cm

Cast ceramic is one of the most elusive and elegant mediums. The white forms portray every element of the design, and the matte surfaces show every nuance of shadow and depth.

"Embouchure" is the french word for the way musicians shape their mouths when they play a wind or brass instrument. This sculpture suggests that flow of air. Invisible energy is realized as a positive, sinuous form.

31. *Nocturne*
    Patinated bronze
    1981, edition 15
    11″ or 27.83 cm

32. *Entrechat*
    Mahogany
    1982
    26″ or 65.78 cm
    Collections: Williams College Museum of Art, Williamstown, Massachusetts

33. *Bouree*
    Mahogany
    1982
    17″ or 43 cm

34. *Camerata*
    Mahogany
    1986/1987
    23″ or 58.19 cm

35. *Cleff VII*
    Mahogany and brass
    1982
    20″ or 50.6 cm

36. *Cadenza*
    Marble
    1981
    18″ or 45.45 cm

37. *Eschelle*
    Ceramic·
    1984
    19″ or 48.07

38. *Poisson D'Or #15*
    Patinated and polished bronze
    1987, edition 15 (9 patina a + 6 patina b)
    10⅜″ or 26.25 cm

39. *Psalma I*
    Patinated and polished bronze
    1985/1986, edition 15 (9 patina a + 6 patina b)
    6″ or 15.18 cm

40. *Concerto for Strings*
    Patinated and polished bronze
    1988, edition 15
    13″ or 32.5 cm

41. *Psalma II*
    Polished bronze
    1986, edition 15 (9 polished + 6 patinated)
    7″ or 17.7 cm

42. *Lullaby*
    Patinated bronze
    1982, edition 15
    9″ or 22.77 cm

43. *Enigmatic Variation #11*
    Mahogany
    1987
    15½″ or 39.22 cm

44. *Eroica*
    Patinated bronze
    1982/1983, edition 15 (9 patina a + 6 patina b)
    23½″ or 59.46 cm
    Collections: Currier Gallery and Museum, Manchester, New Hampshire

45. *Poisson D'Or #14*
    Mahogany polychrome
    1986
    12½″ or 31.63 cm

46. *Enigmata*
    Patinated bronze
    1985, edition 15 (9 patina a + 6 patina b)
    11¾″ or 29.72 cm

It takes about six months to make a typical work in bronze at the foundry. There is a true combination of modern high-technology and old-world craftsmanship. The process is ceramic-shell lost-wax, so the pieces are hollow and exceedingly accurate, right down to an artist's fingerprints. A rubber and plaster master mold generates wax duplicates of the artist's original prototype. Each edition wax is coated inside and out with a ceramic shell mold. The wax form is then melted/burned out and, in its place, molten bronze is poured into the negative space within the shell. When the bronze cools, the ceramic is then removed and the finishing process is begun.

Each sculpture is made singly, passing through the hands of about two dozen foundry specialists trained to work on these pieces. No artist has the full expertise to make such sophisticated abstract forms, and few have access to the extensive equipment and facilities required. It is a symbiotic relationship with the artist contributing aesthetic input along the way. The mutual goal is to create a unique work which respects the soul of the artist and the technical aid of the foundry staff.

David Chamberlain

1949 Born in Canton, Ohio August 11.

EDUCATION

1977 MFA, University of Pennsylvania; sculpture.
1972 Colorado College, Teaching Studio Art Institute.
1971 BA, Princeton University; architecture & design.

SELECTED EXHIBITIONS

SOLO

McKissick Museum, Columbia, SC.
Renjeau Gallery, Concord, MA.
Retrospective: Art Complex Museum,
 Duxbury, MA.
Pucker Safrai Gallery, Boston, MA.
Gibson Gallery, SUNY at Potsdam, NY.
Arlene McDaniel Galleries, Simsbury, CT.
Lyme Academy of Fine Arts, Old Lyme, CT.
Gallerie Obussier, Nantucket, MA.
Pucker Safrai Gallery, Boston, MA.
New Acquisitions Gallery, Syracuse, NY.
Everson Museum of Art, Syracuse, NY.
Concord Art Association, Concord, MA.
Gallery on the Green, Lexington, MA.

GROUP

Joanne Lyon Galleries, Aspen, CO.
Renjeau Gallery, Concord, MA.
Art Gala '87, Kansas City, MO.
National Invitational Sculpture Show,
 Hartford, CT.
Texas Interfaith Exhibition, Austin, TX.
CAFA Exhibition, New Britain Museum of
 American Art, CT.
Contemporary Sculpture at Chesterwood,
 Stockbridge, MA.
Pucker Safrai Gallery, Boston, MA.
Arlene McDaniel Galleries, Simsbury, CT.
Gallery on the Green, Lexington, MA.
Saratoga Gallery of Fine Art, Saratoga, NY.
New Acquisitions Gallery, Syracuse, NY.
Main Street Gallery, Nantucket, MA.
Richard Green Gallery, Guilford, CT.
Mitchell Museum of Art, Mt Vernon, IL.
Kendal Gallery, Wellfleet, MA.
Grimaldis Gallery, Baltimore, MD.
International Sculpture Show, Boston, MA.
Institute of Contemporary Art, Philadelphia, PA.

VISITING ARTIST

Bard College/Simons Rock, Bentley College,
Brandeis University, Colorado College, Emerson College,
Harvard University, Mount Holyoke College, Lyme
Academy of Fine Art, Pine Manor College, Syracuse
University.

PRESENTATIONS

"All Things Considered", National Public Radio,
WBZ-TV, Boston; WCNY-TV Syracuse; WNPI-TV
Watertown, NY, WSBK-TV Boston.

COLLECTIONS

MUSEUMS

Currier Gallery & Museum, Manchester, NH.
Art Complex Museum, Duxbury, MA.
Jewett Museum of Art, Wellesley, MA.
McKissick Museum of Art, Columbia, SC.
Nelson Museum of Art, Kansas City, MO.
Williams College Museum, Williamstown, MA.
Colorado Springs Fine Arts Center, Colorado Springs, CO.
Smith College Museum, Northampton, MA.
The Delaware Museum of Art, Wilmington DE.
Gibson Gallery & Museum, SUNY, NY.
Johnson Museum of Art, Ithaca, NY.
Muskegon Museum of Art, Muskegon, MI.
Wadsworth Athenaeum, Hartford, CT.
Fine Arts Center at Cheekwood, Nashville, TN.

INSTITUTIONS

Bank of America, Boston, MA.
Fidelity Ventures & Assocs., Boston, MA.
Kepner-Tregor Co., Princeton, NJ.
Opinion Research Co., Princeton, NJ.
Price, Waterhouse & Co., Greenwich, CT.
Spencer, Fane & Browne, Kansas City, MO.
Trinity Episcopal Church, Watertown, NY.
Yankelovich, Skelly & White, Stamford, CT.
St. Joseph's Hospital, Lexington, KY.
Carney, Sandoe & Assocs., Boston, MA,
Hilton Walker & Co., Newton, MA.
Monsanto, Brussels, Belgium.
PAR Assocs, Inc., Boston, MA.
Shughart, Thompson & Kilroy, Kansas City, MO.
Temple Society of Concord, Syracuse, NY.
Weston, Willard & Patrick, Boston, MA.
Eliot Bank, Boston, MA.

AWARDS AND COMMISSIONS

1987 *Ballette'*, Ensign-Bickford Corp., Simsbury, CT.
1986 *Torus*, Stratus Computer, Inc. Marlboro, MA.
1985 *Rondella*, BNWC, Brandeis, Waltham, MA.
1983 *Viole, Ayre*, Asset Mgt., Inc., Essex, CT.
1981 *Cantata*, Horn Library, Babson, Wellesley, MA.
1982 Videotape, *Search for Perfection*, American Film
 Festival, NY.
 Red Ribbon.
1975–77 Scholarship; Venture Fund Grant, Office of
 Provost, University of Pennsylvania.
1971 Art Center and Program; Purnell School.
 Who's Who in American Art, Who's Who
 (World).

PROFESSIONAL

1976–77 Artist-in-Residence; Arts College House,
 University of Pennsylvania.
1973–74 Chairperson; Department of Performing & Visual
 Arts, Purnell.

COMPOSITIONS

1976 *Selections*, (poetry).
1974 *Bits and Pieces*, (musical prod.).

ARRANGEMENTS

1974- *Cahoots*, (quartet).
1972–74 *All Good Children*, (octet).
1971–72 *Canto Ergo Sum*, (sextet).
1967–71 *Princeton Footnotes*.